THE ART OF COARSE ACTING

Michael Green's Comic Classic

‖SAMUEL FRENCH‖

samuelfrench.co.uk

First published by Hutchinson & Co Publishers Ltd 1964.
Reprinted three times (Arrow Books edition 1970)
Reprinted 1975, 1976, 1980, 1985, 1988, 1994, 2014

Plays by MICHAEL GREEN
published and licensed by Samuel French

Four Plays for Coarse Actors
Streuth
I Fornicazione
A Collier's Tuesday Tea
All's Well That Ends As You Like It

The Coarse Acting Show 2
Moby Dick
The Cherry Sisters
Last Call for Breakfast
Henry the Tenth (Part Seven)

The Third Great Coarse Acting Show
A Fish in Her Kettle by David Pearson
Present Slaughter by Jane Dewey and Don Starkey
The Vagabond Prince by Simon Brett with music and lyrics
by John Gould
Stalag 69 by Michael Green
Julius and Cleopatra by Michael Green

Coarse Acting Strikes Back
Trapped
Oedocles, King of Thebes
Pride at Southhanger Park by Rupert Bean
Cinderella

Umlaut Prince of Düsseldorf

Haggard – An Entertainment by Eric Chappell based on
characters created by Michael Green

FIND PERFECT PLAYS TO PERFORM AT
www.samuelfrench.co.uk/perform

CONTENTS

ACKNOWLEDGEMENTS

Although the Questors Theatre, Ealing, have tried to deny it, the author is very grateful to them for help with the illustrations.

The author is also grateful to the actors' trade union Equity for not expelling him.

Permission to quote from George Bernard Shaw's work was granted by The Society of Authors on behalf of the Bernard Shaw Estate.

Permission to quote from T.S. Eliot's *The Family Reunion* was granted by Faber and Faber Ltd as publishers.

Permission to quote from *Summoned by Bells* by John Betjeman was granted by John Murray (Publishers) Ltd.

The author would like to thank his wife Christine for her great help in producing this new edition and also David and Sonia Pearson for photographic research.

ILLUSTRATIONS

In photograph section:

All-purpose Coarse expression (female).
How to steal a scene, though unconscious.
Traditional way of killing.
Wrong way to die.
Correct method of dying.
Wrong way to take a prompt.
Basic all-purpose Coarse costume (female).
The author wearing all-purpose Coarse costume (male).
The man on the left has read this book.
The girl on the left has also read this book.
If production photographs look like this the company are Coarse actors.
A Coarse actor press-ganged into playing a Shakespearean clown.
Stock Coarse character.
A scene from a classic tragedy.
An unfortunate accident in a sword fight.
On the Coarse stage dying people speak louder and longer.
Don't get carried away to draw out the sword.
What happens if you are rude to the wardrobe mistress.
This man married the wardrobe mistress.
This production was nearly spoiled.
One of Shakespeare's greatest scenes.
Pity about the infant prince. He got trodden on.

Line drawings

I dedicate this book to:
The Masque Theatre, Northampton
The Crescent Theatre, Birmingham
Richmond Shakespeare Society
and
The Questors Theatre, Ealing
all of whom survived me.

ABOUT THE AUTHOR

Michael Green was born in Leicester, England in 1927 and started writing as a reporter on the local newspaper. He has never been a lumberjack or sold hot dogs. Since publication in 1960 of his first book, *The Art of Coarse Rugby*, he has been a full-time author specialising in telling the grim truth about such pursuits as golf, sailing, drinking, moving and acting, and his books have sold over a million copies world-wide. In 1977 he took a company of amateurs to The Edinburgh Festival with a stage version of *The Art of Coarse Acting* called *The Coarse Acting Show*, and it was hailed as the comedy hit of the season. Two years later, *The Coarse Acting Show 2* was awarded a "Fringe First" at The Edinburgh Festival and then transferred to London's West End for three months. But Michael remained modest. "I have a great deal to be modest about," he said.

FOREWORD

Why a foreword? Why indeed. Why must the show go on? Well the show need not necessarily go on, as I have tried to show in succeeding pages, but the Foreword is going on, simply for the purpose of thanking all those who have ever acted with me for their part in some extraordinary experiences. One of the most enjoyable things about my sordid acting career has been the friendships I have made, and I hope some of the friendships survive this book. Some, I am afraid, will not. While on the subject of the wonderful friendships one makes in the theatre I should like to say that I publicly forgive the man in Birmingham who borrowed several pounds off me just before he went on stage and who was never seen again; and the person at Ealing who has got all my make-up, including the vital materials for Stock Character No. 3.

Perhaps I might also take the opportunity of appealing for the return of my complete Shakespeare, the coin which I used to twist in my tights, my braces and – but why go on? The list is endless.

Michael Green

AUTHOR'S INTRODUCTION:
50 YEARS OF COARSE ACTING

When this book was first published in 1964 the Editorial Director of Hutchinson Publishers said, "I must warn you Michael, we have never successfully sold a book on amateur acting." So it is rather gratifying to be writing a new introduction to celebrate half a century in print, latterly with Samuel French. There have been umpteen reprints and the phrase Coarse Acting for a misplaced performance seems to have passed into the language; at any rate, it was the answer to a clue in *The Times* Crossword and a question in a BBC TV quiz.

One difficulty with a long lasting book is that life changes over fifty years. When the book was first published in 1964 "God Save the Queen" was still played before Performances, the Lord Chamberlain censored scripts and audiences smoked throughout the show, although there was no interruption from mobile phones, as they hadn't been invented. Telegrams filled the dressing-room, sometimes with a dubious message from a jealous actor who hadn't been cast such as:

GOOD LUCK DESPITE DREADFUL DRESS REHEARSAL – RODNEY

Sound effects were either produced live or played on tape or vinyl gramophone records. I must be one of the few left who has shaken a sheet of tin to imitate thunder or turned the handle of a wind machine.

But Coarse Acting is more than the mere mechanics of production. It's been around as long as drama. Shakespeare wrote the first Coarse Acting play with the mechanicals' efforts to stage the tragedy of Pyramus and Thisbe in *A Midsummer Night's Dream*, as hilarious today as any modern spoof. Contemporary companies have their Bottom the Weaver and Peter Quince. So although I've amended the book to remove some of the more glaring anachronisms, too much revision would be out of place, rather like putting an outboard motor in *Three Men in a Boat*.

A later development has been stage versions of Coarse Acting (deliberate productions, that is, not accidental ones). This started off with Coarse Acting competitions at The Questors Theatre, Ealing, London, in which various teams competed in displays of theatrical mayhem and the idea spread. At The Questors, the Royal Shakespeare Company entered a team consisting of Roger Rees and Tony Pedley and performed the murder scene from *Julius Caesar*, with the difference that Caesar became incensed at being painfully stabbed by Brutus, and, snatching the dagger, chased him round the stage and out of the auditorium. Something not very different had actually happened at the same theatre a few years previously when a stage sword fight finished up as a genuine brawl. In a contest held to raise funds for the new Salisbury Playhouse, the National Theatre sent down a production notable for a remarkable performance by the butler, who aged ten years every time he entered the room, so he started up about thirty and ended up about ninety.

All this culminated in shows based on the book. In 1977 I took *The Coarse Acting Show* to the Edinburgh Fringe Festival with a company from The Questors, and it was well received. The show simply portrayed an evening with an incompetent amateur company. Two years later we put on a sequel at Edinburgh, *The Coarse Acting Show Two*, and this transferred to the Shaftesbury Theatre, London, the first (official) appearance of Coarse Acting in the West End. Two more shows followed and all four are published by Samuel French, forming natural companions to this book.

Incidentally, The Questors' 1980 competition spawned a macabre coincidence. Timothy West very generously agreed to adjudicate and chose as the winner a play in which a character was supposed to cut his wrist accidentally on stage and gradually sink into unconsciousness. A week later exactly the same thing happened to Timothy. Playing in his one-man show *Beecham* he cut himself on a broken glass, struggled to continue, failed and went to hospital to have twenty stitches in his hand while the performance was abandoned. Which only goes to prove truth can be as strange as fiction.

If I thought the original volume exhausted the subject how wrong I was. I've received shoals of letters over the years detailing fresh stage horrors, such as the experience of an actor who rammed his spear through a scenery flat, wounding a passing ASM. A girl wrote to say she wrecked the college *Pygmalion* by getting her parasol jammed in a crack in the stage, where it stuck so firmly they had to leave it for the rest of the play. Some students from Cambridge University sent details of a club they had founded for Coarse lighting operators, The Shaft of Darkness Society.

HRH The Prince of Wales visited *Coarse Acting Two* at The Shaftesbury Theatre and revealed he experienced Coarse Acting at school, where an English master, having successfully put on *Richard III*, produced Gilbert and Sullivan in the same manner, with disastrous results. HRH also recalled a royal tour when a female dancer curtsied so deeply at the end of a performance she injured her back and had to be carried from the stage frozen in a curtsy position. My own experiences have broadened too. When I wrote the original book I never dreamed a few years later I would fall off-stage at a dress rehearsal, break a leg, dislocate my elbow, and be carried into the casualty ward of the local hospital dressed as an eighteenth-century pirate. It was the annual Christmas romp and the costume spared nothing. I was dressed in a coat and knee-breeches of the period and heavily made-up to look evil. One eye was hidden by a patch. My right arm terminated in a steel hook. The left leg was strapped up and a wooden leg attached to the knee. A parrot was sewn on one shoulder and a dagger stuck from my blood covered chest.

The nurse's surprise may be imagined but she controlled herself nobly and started to deal with the stage wounds while ignoring the real ones. After an unsuccessful attempt to make the parrot fly away she grabbed the dagger and pulled but it wouldn't come.

At this point she sensibly decided to send for the doctor who arrived all bustle and efficiency and disguised his surprise at the apparition on the bed with an effort.

"And what seems to be the trouble?" he said with masterly understatement.

"It's my leg," I explained, pawing the air feebly with my hook in the general direction of the lower limbs.

He looked down at the bottle-shaped wooden peg. "Mmmm", he muttered, "it's not a very good one. I'll make an appointment for you to have a new one fitted tomorrow."

But enough. We have all suffered in the cause of drama, and the more true the story the more unbelievable the experience. I just hope this revised volume gives as much pleasure as the original version appeared to do.

Michael Green
London 2014

PROLOGUE

(Preferably spoken by Mrs Bracegirdle)

Now doth the Muse of Drama stir this age
And thousands hear the lure of the stage.
Then see the truckling city clerk at night
Transformed into a royal and noble sight.
Bedecked in tinplate armour watch him tower,
A swelling monarch for his petty hour.
The humble typist sheds her office weeds
And lo! We have a Carmen straight from Leeds!
Fear not, all amateurs are not the same,
Some Little Theatres higher standards claim,
And hold with fervour nigh obsessional
That amateurs are equal to professional.
Yet amateur, profession'l, clown or Lear,
Someone must bear the message, grasp the spear.
With crêpe hair all askew, a parley hold,
Or tell the guests that dinner's getting cold.
It is for these poor servants of the Muse,
Coarse Actors all, that I this volume choose.
A dedication make, both brief and short
To those with cardboard spears at Agincourt.

1

An Introduction to Coarse Acting

"I had as lief the town-crier spoke my lines..." Hamlet

**What is a Coarse Actor? – the unhappiness with Askew
– the Unpleasantness at Birmingham – instant Shakespeare
– a clanger in Wagner**

Many years ago I was in an amateur production of a play with a friend called Askew. He is one of those people who would like to be successful on stage but has no intention of doing anything about it. Whenever he walks on he seems to be wearing stilts inside his trousers. Together we have wrecked many a carefully planned production.

In this play four of us had a whole scene in which we were merely required to sit at the back of the stage and play cards, occasionally making some interjection or other. One night, to while away the time, we played a real game in which we became completely immersed, while the main action continued in front of us.

The only snag was Askew had not bothered to learn his lines but simply wrote them on the back of his playing cards. This was fine until he accidentally played the card with his lines on and I trumped it and shuffled it into the pack.

There was about fifteen seconds before the cue came. Playing cards flew in all directions and half the pack went under the table where Askew crawled on his hands and knees looking for the vital card. The audience ignored the main characters and concentrated on us, thinking something desperate was about to happen under the card table. Eventually the cue came with three of us still under the table, there was a horrid pause and then with a cry of triumph Askew found his card and bellowed forth his two miserable lines from a kneeling position.

It was only afterwards that he realised he had found the wrong card and said the lines from the next act, which made gibberish of the plot. Moral: always write your lines on an ace.

That is Coarse Acting.

Coarse in this sense is nothing to do with "crude"; it is the way things get done in life by ordinary people as opposed to the experts. Thus, we are taught that yachtsmen are gallant seadogs using strange, marine language, whereas in *The Art of Coarse Sailing* I define a Coarse Sailor as one who, in a crisis, forgets all that nautical rubbish about port and starboard and shouts, "For God's sake turn left, you fool."

As for that legend about rugby players being young giants with thighs like oak trees and impervious to pain, that may be true for some, but down on the local park there will be plenty of shivering sales reps praying for the game to finish so the agony will cease. Hence the definition of Coarse Rugby: "A game played by fewer than fifteen a side, at least half of whom never wanted to turn out in the first place."

So what is a Coarse Actor? (I use the word to include actress.) It's difficult to find an all-embracing description, but since they often have trouble with their words a good definition might be: one who can remember the lines but not the order in which they come. It is perhaps not an entirely satisfactory definition and a friend suggests a Coarse Actor is one who can remember the pauses but not the line.

However, that definition falls down because most Coarse Actors don't have any pauses. They regard their lines rather as a machine gunner regards a belt of ammunition: something to be shot off in the vague direction of the enemy and then replaced as rapidly as possible. Other definitions which may prove accurate are:

One who knows when to come on-stage but not where.

One whose eyebrows are attached to their feet
(so every facial expression involves the whole body as well).

One who limps on both legs simultaneously.

One who acts with their elbows. (This is quite common.

On the Coarse stage an injured leg is usually accompanied by a distorted arm on the same side which goes up and down with the leg. Some actors and actresses even *sneer* with their elbows, the joint being raised along with the side of the mouth. Try it sometime in a mirror.)

One who plays all parts exactly the same.

One who knows everyone else's lines better than their own (that is certainly true of Askew).

One who remembers the last play better than the one they're actually in. (Since writing that I've met somebody who knew the *next* play better than the one they were in.)

An irate treasurer of a theatre group wrote angrily, "Surely a Coarse Actor is one who makes the leading lady pregnant and then fails to pay their subscription," but I feel this is a special instance. In any case, it is not clear whether he objected to the pregnancy or failure to pay the sub.

Certainly, one of the infallible signs Coarse Drama is going on is that the traditional roles of actor and audience are reversed. The actor is being himself while the audience are playing a part, heavily pretending to enjoy the show, struggling to laugh at unfunny jokes and so on. Watching a bad show can be more exhausting than three hours on stage.

There are many sides to Coarse Acting. It isn't just forgetting lines or hamming it up. One of its most common forms is the cliché-performance, like those dreadful small parts in Hollywood costume epics, not to mention Shakespearean crowds. Some Coarse Actors are quite good, but accident prone. Even famous players are not immune. One is said to have had a terrible experience in *Tamburlaine* at the National during the scene when four captive kings are forced to pull his chariot. With a cry of "On to Persepolis ho!" he cracked his whip and they strained mightily, only to find the chariot had seized up (it was one of those over-realistic National Theatre props that weigh more than the original). Once more they tried and failed, whereupon he leaned over the front and hissed angrily, "Stop pulling and lift the bastard!"

For many Coarse Actors, pistols never fire, doors stick, buttons come off at vital moments. They will come on stage, bringing down the scenery by forcing a door and then march confidently round the set revealing that their trousers are undone and they have coloured underwear, oblivious to the fact the rest of the cast are cringing with embarrassment. But they have a pathetic belief the audience never noticed. "Believe me old chap, the audience never noticed a thing" is the hallmark of the Coarse Actor.

Another group can never be natural. They have to stand out at all costs. They seem to have a terrible compulsion to be maimed. Whole armies limp before they even get into battle. Complete villages of peasants – men and women – go hoppity-hop.

Perhaps it all starts in youth when, in a moustache made from burnt cork, the trembling infant is pushed reluctantly on stage to mouth his halting lines while the girl opposite bursts into tears for no reason at all. It is then the child discovers, that awful though he is, several hundred people are paying attention to him. It is too much for the immature mind.

Certainly the tendency to limp starts early. I remember a local Nativity play in which the Three Wise Men (all aged seven) entered in apparently the last stages of arthritis. As I said to the headmistress, "It doesn't say in the Bible the Three Wise Men were club-footed," but she didn't see the joke. But then school plays are particularly disaster-ridden. They are the only form of theatre where the cast are liable to be sick all over the stage.

Naturally, most Coarse Actors are amateurs, although with the growth of "professional" fringe companies in which nobody gets paid anything except a share of the loss, I'm not sure this is as true as it was. But Coarse professionals don't usually survive long. Even so, there are plenty around, like the elderly chap who was cast for a television programme I wrote. It was subtle piece of writing, of which I was rather proud. All he had to do was spit. If I remember correctly the dialogue went something like this:

ANNOUNCER But there were those who said the whole voyage was useless.

Cut to close-up of **HOUSEWIFE**.

HOUSEWIFE Seems silly to me.

Cut to close-up of **BUSINESSMAN.**

BUSINESSMAN They'll never do it.

Cut to close-up of **OLD SAILOR.**

OLD SAILOR *(spits)*

Good stuff, eh? Eventually we got to the telerecording and the director warned everyone that this was costing umpteen pounds a second, so treat it as a performance boys and girls, and good luck, etc., etc. The cameras started and all went well until five minutes from the end, when they cut to the old sailor. There was a thick silence for some five seconds and then he simply said, "I'm terribly sorry, old boy, I've forgotten what you wanted me to do."

I don't think he ever got another part. They did not ask me to write any more scripts.

Amateur acting is, however, littered with ex-professionals. It is never quite plain as to why they are ex. When asked why they quit the stage they usually have some fantastic yarn about having quarrelled with Cameron Mackintosh over a major West End role.

I once acted with an old pro who had travelled all over the globe. When he performed Shylock in Bulgaria the audience hissed. He thought he was going to be lynched until someone explained that hissing is a sign of approval over there.

This old chap had a sort of *droit de seigneur* on all our Shakespearean "heavies". The first time I met him he was in the *Merchant of Venice,* in which he was Shylock, of course, and I was astonished at the first rehearsal when he started to make a series of moves that bore no relation to the set, since one move consisted of tottering brokenly up a huge staircase, and we didn't have a staircase – he was supposed to go off left behind a curtain.

The director, rather understandably, protested.

"Laddie," came the reply, "you can't teach an old dog new tricks. These moves were good enough for Sir Barry Jackson and they ought to be good enough for you."

But there are certain basic assumptions about a professional production – such as usually having a full cast – that rule out the best in Coarse drama. In fact it is one of the hallmarks that, in the same way as Coarse Rugby or Cricket sides never have a full team, a Coarse play never has a full company.

I shall not easily forget a production of *Henry V* which coincided with an influenza epidemic. We were always one player short, in any case. It was a sort of floating gap, filled each night with whomever could get into the messenger's costume in time. If nobody achieved this then the stage manager bellowed something from the wings and the King edged his way across and held converse with an invisible man.

The epidemic, however, made things much worse. No one knew what part he would have to play next. Mysterious messages would be left at the office during the day such as "Mr Green, someone rang to say you are Lord Scroop tonight. Does that make sense?"

Worse still, you would turn up at the theatre all unsuspecting, and be making-up as Bardolph or some such harmless role, when the stage manager would approach, thrust a heap of armour into your arms and say: "Bert's ill. You're doubling the Earl of Essex tonight."

Since there was no time to learn the appropriate lines, one came on stage, usually from the wrong side, groping about in ill-fitting armour and trying to read from the script at the same time.

It is hardly surprising that as a result I died after a sword fight which I should have won. Actually it was a little awkward because the other chap also died and we both tottered away clutching our vitals without having touched each other.

There was a nasty silence and the audience became restive. I managed to roll over and look at my script, which was pasted inside my shield, and saw I was supposed to make a speech over my opponent's bleeding corpse. Fortunately I had enough presence of mind to stagger to my feet in a manner which suggested I was merely winded and say a quick epitaph over my enemy (in view of the delay I cut the real speech and just muttered something about dust and a heap of bones).

The climax came when even with everyone doubling two or three parts there just weren't enough men to go round. The only thing left to do was to cut the play as we went along, omitting those on the sick list.

It was the quickest performance of *Henry V* on record. Whole episodes of English history vanished. I don't think the Battle of Agincourt ever took place. In the end we discovered we had done it in under 90 minutes, which as far as I know is a world record.

Yet however much Shakespeare suffers at the hands of Coarse Actors, they suffer for him too.

For me and many others a Shakespeare play is a mad whirl. I begin by rushing on stage and bellowing a line like "My Lord, the French, with ill-advised speed do..." I am never allowed to go further because the King interrupts with an endless speech about what he's going to do to those Frogs, rebels, Scots, etc.

For the rest of the evening I rush through the dressing-room, changing beards and costumes every so often as I try to carry a spear for both sides, until finally, clad in insanitary and evil-smelling armour I am spitted to death in the last battle, and die grovelling on a dusty floor with the hole in my tights exposed to the stalls.

Sometimes I die twice, or even three times. Coarse Actors are little better than sword-fodder.

Another common part for Coarse Actors is that of Shakespearean clown, or more often, assistant clown. Unfortunately, humour has changed a great deal in 400 years and Elizabethan comics can be the unfunniest parts ever written. Just compare the hilarious lines Shakespeare gives to his serious characters ("Ah me, my uncle's spirit is in these stones, now heaven take my soul and England take my bones" as he writes in *King John*) with the stuff he dishes out to the comedians.

Much of this is incomprehensible to a modern audience so the Coarse Actor will find himself trying to wring laughter from a speech something like, "By the Mass, ye are as addle-pated as a tailor that hath got his horns at Spitalfelds, birlady and God's sonties, and if ye are not, let me be stuffed with a girt gurdy thuggett and condemned to listen to a quondam thrasonical catch, aye marry fart and amen."

These lines are usually spoken in a low growl, accompanied by a funny walk and placing fingers on the forehead like horns every time the word is mentioned, which is about every other line. Sometimes the actor will resort to desperate measures to break the stony silence that greets him, adding grimaces, winks, belches and farts. Fortunately the lines are so dreadful it does not matter if one mixes them up or even forgets them completely. I once played the clown in John Marston's *The Malcontent*, where I had the side-splitting speech: "He hath sore eyes...for the roots of the horns are in the eyeballs, which is why the horn of a cuckold is as tender as his eye."

On at least half the performances I said, "The roots of the eyeballs are in the horns" but far from spoiling the speech it usually got a laugh. I think it made as much sense as the original, at any rate.

Some day I should like to run a competition to find the unfunniest clown in Shakespeare. There's a lot of choice, starting with Macbeths's incomprehensible drunken porter ("...here's an English tailor come hither for stealing out of French hose..." ho, ho, ho). Nobody can make me believe even the groundlings laughed at them, unless, as I suspect, the lines were enlivened by rude gestures.

It's always a mystery how Shakespeare, who created immortal comic dialogue and situations with characters from Falstaff to Malvolio or Dogberry, should apparently lose his touch with the clowns. A former member of the Royal Shakespeare Company told me the most terrible moment of his career was when he got a letter asking him to play Touchstone. He immediately wrote back and asked if fifty per cent of the lines could be cut.

Top-class directors take immense care over the clown scenes, bringing out every morsel of humour and making extensive use of funny business. I never cease to admire how players at the RSC or National manage to make even the most obscure lines appear sense and be amusing too. Suddenly the clowns really are funny. But, alas, lesser known directors are at their worst with clowns. They refuse to cut them; they don't know how to direct them; so they leave them to their own devices but still insist they ought to be hilarious. Or they may allege the clown isn't meant to be funny, he's meant to be pathetic.

During a production of *Twelfth Night,* in which I played Fabian, the director carefully explained Feste was the elderly clown on his way out, which was why he wasn't funny, and Fabian was the up and coming replacement. I pointed out Fabian was even less funny than Feste, but I could not convince him. I remember one line in particular:

"Sowter will cry out upon't for all this, though it be rank as a fox."

Every time we came to that in rehearsal I said, "Look, surely you don't really believe that's funny, do you?" and the director would assume an air of pitying superiority and say: "It's simply the way you're saying it."

I tried every way of saying that wretched line. I said, "Sowter will *cry* out on it," and I said, "*Sowter* will cry out on it," and I said, "Sowter will cry *out* on it," and it still fell on the audience like a lump of suet pudding, until one evening I delivered it as usual and there was a great shout of laughter from the back of the hall.

For just a moment I thought I had triumphed over the Bard, when I realised that there was something familiar about the laughter. I glanced off stage and saw that the stage manager was not in his seat. He had collected every spare person, crept in at the back of the auditorium and organised a claque for the line. After that the real audience became convinced they were missing something and laughed in all sorts of unexpected places. The only person who didn't think it hilarious was the director.

One is tempted to the theory that Shakespeare himself was a Coarse Actor. At any rate he was certainly experienced in their ways, as Hamlet's advice to the players shows: "And let not those that play the clowns say more than is set down for them." It seems to me quite obvious that Will Kemp and one or two others had got tired of those corny old jokes about sowter and horns and French tailors and started putting in some real gags. And after playing some of the clowns' parts I must say I don't blame them.

Because standards have risen so much, it might be thought Coarse Acting wouldn't happen any more except in some remote village hall. But it was at one of the most prominent amateur theatres in Britain that an actor lost his way in a blackout, fell off the stage and found himself groping around blindly in the aisle. An attendant thought he was a member of the audience and asked, "Do you want the toilet?" and the actor replied, "No, I am the Duke of Burgundy and I want to get out of here."

Meanwhile the stage manager decided to send out a search party drawn from the English army; the audience were startled to find men carrying swords prowling round the stalls, where they discovered the dazed Duke and led him to safety through an emergency exit.

Fortunately, many thought it was part of the production. Indeed, somebody wrote in the company newsletter, "The director's brilliant use of the auditorium as part of the acting area was an object lesson in total theatre and the scene where the Duke of Burgundy takes refuge in the stalls, before being dragged by soldiers to his doom, was a moment of sheer inspiration and the climax of his emotional decay."

It was, by the way, at the same theatre that Osric waved his sword to start the famous duel in *Hamlet* and got it stuck in the proscenium arch. As a matter of fact I was the culprit and unfortunately it was a rapier with a bent point so I couldn't get it out. I felt a complete idiot tugging away while the scene went on. It completely destroyed Hamlet's death – everyone was looking at me. I just had to leave it hanging for the curtain call. The director has not invited me to tea since. I visited Laertes in Australia recently, and it was still on his mind.

In fact the higher up the scale one goes, the greater the opportunities that seem to arise for Coarse Acting because in a bad production so much goes wrong, one thing more or less is not noticed, whereas in a well-staged piece any lone mayhem stands out like a beacon.

My first experience of this was when I joined the famous Crescent Theatre (the Unpleasantness in Birmingham). Previous acting had been limited to small groups, so naturally I was anxious to do well, and rather frightened of their reputation.

My first part was as a Russian peasant in *Wolves and Sheep* by Ostrovsky. I came on with other peasants in the first scene and afterwards we changed into overalls and were used as scene-shifters. As we used to get in the way, smoking and chattering in the wings, the stage manager told us to clear out and go in the pub over the road until needed. We rather forgot about time over there until the First Peasant looked at his watch and said, "We'd better hurry, there's only a minute to the change."

We ran across the road and into the wings just as a burst of applause rang out. The First Peasant picked up a table and rushed on stage with it, while I followed with a potted fern.

At that moment I realised with horror that the curtain was still up. The applause had been for an actor's exit.

Fortunately I wasn't properly on stage. Only my leg was visible, suspended in mid-air around a piece of scenery. I slowly lowered the leg and wormed it backwards out of sight.

The First Peasant wasn't so lucky. He did not realise his mistake until he was about to deposit the table on stage. It was then he became aware of a ghastly silence and a rustling in the audience. I must say, you couldn't blame the actors for stopping. It is rather upsetting when two men in overalls dash on in the middle of a scene and start heaving furniture about.

With great presence of mind the First Peasant put down the table, bowed and walked off stage with as much dignity as he could muster. There was one of *those* silences and then the scene dragged on. It did this with some difficulty, as now the stage was blocked with a huge table which wasn't supposed to be there.

Later, Coarse Theatre stalked me on to the professional stage. In one of Scotland's best theatres, at Inverness, my one-man show was obliterated in mid-performance when suddenly all the lights turned red and switched to the other side of the stage, leaving me bleating helplessly. I moved into the lights but they slowly turned purple and went out. A distraught operator told me afterwards a power surge affected the computer and the board reverted to sunset in Vienna (they'd just had a musical). Still, as one of the audience said, it was the funniest part of the show.*

No, Coarse Theatre flourishes everywhere, from the humblest hall to the greatest theatres. It was at the Old Vic, no less, that I saw a death scene so ridiculous the audience laughed and somebody cried "Encore". I have even seen Coarse Theatre at The Royal Opera House, Covent Garden. At least, I don't think it was deliberate that Siegfried's sword broke and he had to go off and fetch another.

Never mind, Siegfried. Nobody has ever paid me umpteen thousands for a performance but I know how you felt. And so do thousands of us.

---

* Actually, I think he said it was the only funny thing in the show, but I hope I misheard.

2

A Coarse Actor's Approach to his Part

"Why do we feel embarrassed, impatient, ill-at-ease, assembled like
amateur actors who have not been assigned their parts? ..."
T.S. Eliot *(The Family Reunion)*

An amusing contest – no need to learn lines – the
Unpleasantness in various places – what happened to
Globovitch – "Are you aware you were abused as a child?"

Of all people engaged in Coarse Drama the actor is by far the most important. The influence of the director or producer is small, and may even be completely negatived by a hostile cast. And while stage managers may force their personality to the notice of the audience by setting the theatre alight, for instance (see Chapter 8), it is the actor who is chiefly responsible for making or breaking the play.

The smallness of the part has no relation to its possibilities. An actor is said to have kippered an entire production of *Macbeth* by running on and saying, "The Queen, my lord, is *not* dead."

In fact, a good way of whiling away time in a dressing-room is to have a competition to invent lines which would bring famous plays to a premature or disastrous conclusion. An old pal always says his ambition is to destroy the rejection scene at the end of *Henry IV, Part Two,* with "Falstaff, old chap, you are right welcome to our coronation". Others which have won a can of beer are, "Hamlet, I am no ghost, the poison missed my ear" and, "The asp is dead". My own best effort was, "Thank you, Professor Higgins, after one lesson I find I can speak perfectly." But the title must surely be taken by, "Hello, here comes Godot."

What are the outstanding characteristics of a Coarse Actor? Firstly I should say a desperate desire to impress. The true one is most anxious to succeed. In reality, though, Coarse Actors will never admit that they have done badly. Law One of Coarse Drama states: "In retrospect all performances are a success." In fact there is always someone who will maintain the show was better than the West End version. Hostile criticism is dismissed as ill-informed – arrogance rules.

An acquaintance found himself quite literally trapped on stage. He couldn't find the way out (it was one of those rather complicated sets). So he simply forced a gap between two flats and squeezed off stage. But when I tackled him afterwards about it he merely said: "Actually, old boy, you needn't worry. The audience didn't notice anything wrong. You merely *thought* there was something wrong because you knew the play."

It is no use telling someone like that he was awful.

Strangely enough, a Coarse Actor firmly believes the stars have nothing to teach him. On a rare visit to the theatre he is quite capable of criticising Dame Judi Dench, despite the fact she moved hardened critics to tears. My friend Askew, for instance, always maintains Sir Laurence Olivier was not a great actor "because of his cold eyes".

"He didn't feel it," said Askew, who has never in his life remembered a line correctly.

One thing is certain: no Coarse Actor ever really improves, although occasionally they may become worse as their limited faculties desert them with age. Training courses are wasted on them. Train one for three years and he will still walk on stage holding up his hands like a bunch of bananas.

A common type are keen, hard-working and utterly incompetent. When they come on stage it is painfully obvious they are trying very hard to act. They make you want to shout out Sam Goldwyn's classic remark to a raw actress, "Don't just do something – stand there!" Others have some superficial competence but are utterly casual about the whole thing, the sort who carry a book at a dress rehearsal. They are merely there for the beer and the company. A third group are both useless and lazy.

Then there are the accident prone, the forgetful, the terrified and the outrageous. Not to mention people with incurable habits, like the girl I knew who pointed at people every time she spoke or the man who stood up every time he had a line.

And it's not entirely confined to the incompetent or amateurs. The best may get contaminated. Even Peter O'Toole's Macbeth in London in the eighties was so outrageous it was described by one Sunday paper as suitable for a Coarse Acting competition.

Fortunately in most amateur productions people are cast not on ability but on reputation. On joining a new company, therefore, it is essential to provide a ready-made reputation as vague as possible ("Actually I haven't done much since my Lear"). If challenged say it was a new play called Leer by a local author. Long-standing members of a society can use the same technique by referring to a vague past period in their lives. "Pinter? How interesting. I first came across him at Oxford." Ignore the fact you were working for a car factory.

Since the amateur stage is the home of fantasy there's little danger of being challenged, especially if you make the lie a big one. The worst actor I have ever played with claimed he used to be at Liverpool Playhouse. Indeed, getting a big part may be less difficult than avoiding one. If one feels an important role would burst the bubble, decline gracefully and hint you might just find time for something less demanding.

But make sure any small part accepted is not peculiar. I shall never forget entering a fringe theatre and finding my best friend *chained to a pillar in the middle of the audience.* Apparently he was tied there half an hour before the play started and not released until the audience had left.

As he was supposed to be part of the play he could not even talk to his friends, but had to keep staring into space as they all kept asking what the matter was and offering him sweets. It was most embarrassing – we didn't know where to look.

Before rehearsals begin one must consider the characterisation and the approach to the part.

In the same way as there are only a few basic jokes, so there are only a few basic parts in Coarse Theatre, which for convenience I have numbered (see chart).

The first thing that will be noticed about the list is that there are no tragic men or women on it. This is because all elderly people are funny on the Coarse stage.

The TV advert has now become the ultimate refuge of Coarse Acting. Beaming clergymen, genial doctors, well-preserved grannies, sanitised babies and long-suffering parents abound in a world free from any connection with reality.

Further, Coarse Actors don't base their performances on modern life or even the modern stage but on how they remember the part being played when they were young (probably in a black and white film). In any case, many plays of Coarse Theatre belong to the era of Agatha Christie, so these old-fashioned characters will be around for a long time.

Talking of cliché performances, there used to be a splendid piece of Coarse Acting, which now seems to have died out. When a character, male or female, wanted to express strong emotion, they put the back of their hand across their mouth and bit it. This was always accompanied by "My God!" whether it was in the script or not ("My God, what have you done to her.") The cast would finish an emotional play with blood streaming down their knuckles. Perhaps today's players will revive the tradition. It was very effective and saved the tiresome bother of having to act.

A special note must be made about the all-purpose Coarse historical small part, citizen, messenger, peasant, etc. For some reason these are all deformed. I do not know why but the example is set even at the best theatres. I've lost count of the gibbering crones and beggars I've seen over the years. If this is a true reflection of Shakespeare's time imagination boggles at what Stratford-upon-Avon High Street must have been like in 1595, full of people bent double, covered in warts, and squawking in peculiar voices.

Coarse cripples even have a special way of holding their sticks – they don't hold them at the top like ordinary cripples, they hold them near the bottom and go around bent double, banging them on the ground, especially the women. Outside of the stage I have never in my life seen a cripple bang a stick on the ground. The females speak in a hoarse croak. Men have a special gruff accent. All have distorted faces and a tendency to add "heh, heh" at the end of their lines (if any).

Ironically, these cripples often have the most urgent messages. I remember a production of *Lorna Doone* in which a messenger came to tell everyone to flee, the dreaded Judge Jeffreys was arriving, and they apparently sent the village idiot. He took ages to hobble across stage and deliver the warning.

Another part which may fall to the Coarse Actor is that of Shakespearean lord or lady. The women are expected to swish their skirts a great deal. There is a special stance for men, which rather looks as if the actor wanted to visit the toilet. The voice is raised an octave and the actor shouts as loudly as possible, as if hailing a ship in a particularly dense fog, and sprinkles the lines with extra syllables, "Condisheeun" for "condition" and so forth.

[Note that the special costume drama stance for courtiers and aristocrats is exactly the same in any play from 500BC onwards, even if the player is only wearing a loin cloth.]

Let me give an example from life of how all this can work out:

Askew put in for a production of *Hamlet* by an enthusiastic new director of a local society. After the reading we went into a pub on the corner and soon afterwards the director came in highly excited, went to Askew and said, "I've got terrific news – I've cast you as Polonius."

Askew took another swig of beer.

"Jolly good," he said, "Stock Character No. 1, I think will meet the case – funny old man. Do you mind if I give the same performance as for Justice Shallow? I rather liked that walk. I've got most of the make-up left as well."

At this point I thought the director was going to burst into tears. Although it wouldn't have been the first time Askew had driven a director to hysteria. After being cast as the boatswain in *The Tempest* he asked, "Do you want me to sew the parrot on the left or the right shoulder?" He claimed later he was joking but I am not so sure.

In the end Askew dropped out of *Hamlet* because the director insisted on his taking a curtain call, whereas he had counted on going off to the pub after being stabbed behind the arras. It

TRADITIONAL ALL-PURPOSE COARSE ACTING CHARACTER CHART

Character	Example	Make-up etc.	Technique	Notes
1 (a) Old man	Polonius	Tramlines Beard	Stoop Gibber Mow Saw Salivate	Ear trumpet?
1 (b) Old woman	Lady Bracknell	See above (beard optional)	Shout	Stick?
2 (a) Young man (upper class)	Jack Worthing	Arch eyebrows	Vacuous laugh	Monocle?
2 (b) Young woman (upper class)	Gwendolen	Wide eyes like snooker balls	Cig holder	No monocle
3 Universal prole	Cleaner Maid Plumber	Distort face	Say "Cor" frequently	Must raise a laugh
4 General Coarse part in classic drama	Peasant Servant Messenger Citizen	Boils	Curvature of the spine	Imbecile Stick Crutch
5 Contemporary gritty drama	Hero	Leave jeans undone	Vomit occasionally Mumble	Orgasm optional

HOW TO USE THE CHART

This is only a basic guide to those characteristics which a Coarse Actor can assume to portray different roles. He or she must first decide whether they are old or young and whether they are upper class or plebeian. Having decided, they can make use of various stock characteristics, of which a few are listed.

Here are some others:
Clergymen: Half-witted, short-sighted, place tips of fingers together and beam at everyone.
Maids: Bob up and down every time they address anyone.
Policemen: Tread like elephants. Do not know where to put helmet.
Female cleaners: Arms akimbo. Cigarette dangles from lower lip.
Authority Figures, such as headmasters: Preface every remark with "Ah..." ("Ah, Cunningham, I wanted to see you about the exam results." NB Headmistresses preface remarks with "Oh..." instead: "Oh, Daphne, I wanted to see you about the hockey team."

This list applies chiefly to the time before *Look Back in Anger* signalled the start of a new era. A contemporary play would be more likely to portray police as corrupt sadists and clergymen wouldn't appear at all unless they'd been unfrocked for a bestial offence.

But stock performances still abound, especially on TV. Examples may be seen in a bad serial nearly every night; even worse are the commercials, where every mum is incredibly patient and merely gives a wry smile as her child pours ink all over the tablecloth.

is sad that so many directors these days will not co-operate in this sort of thing, and perhaps as important as a black list of parts is a black list of directors. I personally have an extensive one. Directors, of course, have their own on which I doubtless figure.

The sort to avoid is the young woman who directed me in some Russian epic. The lines were the usual Russian remarks, "Shall I put some more logs on the stove?" and the part was plainly a sub-section of Stock Character No. 4 (all-purpose) with foreign overtones. A clear case for one rehearsal.

In fact I was not going to turn up until the night before the dress rehearsal, because there really is not much point in hanging around a draughty hall all evening simply for the privilege of saying "Shall I put some more logs on the stove?" However, the director insisted that everyone attended all the rehearsals. We had to discuss our parts with her and she made us watch the scenes in which we weren't called so we knew what it was all about. We even had to have discussions about what we had for breakfast and what the characters' parents were like.

Now a true Coarse Actor will not put up with this. I am proud to say that in ninety per cent of the plays in which I have performed I have never known what happened at either the end or the beginning. If I am not called early on I am in the bar until the curtain goes up, and if I've finished before the end I'm in the pub when the curtain falls.

And these weeks of endless rehearsal taught me nothing new. All the middle-class characters sat around saying lines like "Five years since Uncle Petrovitch died", and then there would be a long pause and someone else would say "Six", and after another long wait someone else would say "And nothing has changed".

They seemed to say the same lines in each scene. I'm glad I was in the cast – it must have been very depressing to watch it.

After three nights they actually got as far as my first entrance (of two). I was ready, winding myself up in the wings, but every time the cue came ("Ah, here comes Globovitch, our aged servant, who has been with us for fifty years") the director gave a childish wail and beat her foot and squeaked, "No, no, dear, you're not feeling that line."

At this point a voice from the wings said, "How much longer is she going on like this?" and there was a further delay while the culprit was reprimanded.

Long past closing time I was still standing there waiting to go on when to my surprise they passed my cue without interruption. I immediately adopted Stock Walk No. 1 (a), i.e. bending double, shaking my head, gnashing gums, mowing, gibbering meaninglessly, etc., etc. I jerked on stage and quavered, "Shall I put some more logs on the stove?"

The familiar wail came from the darkness out front.

"No, no, Michael darling. You do see what's wrong, don't you?"

Well, I didn't, but I pretended to humour her and I said yes, and went out and did it again.

The reaction was even worse.

"No, Michael. Listen. You do understand there's a storm going on?"

"Yes."

"There will be a howling of wind and the noise of rain on the roof."

"Yes."

"And an orchestra of serfs will be playing on the balcony."

"Yes."

"And you are a man who has been a friend of the family for fifty years, so you know that some of them are deaf."

"Yes."

"So you do see what I'm getting at, don't you?"

"No."

I hoped she would have a fit, but after breathing heavily for a moment she simply shrieked, "I want you to bloody well speak louder."

The outburst did little good because I went into a deep sulk and boomed my lines so loudly for the rest of rehearsal that the female lead said I had given her a headache.

A true Coarse Actor will always be on guard against the efforts of directors like that to read too much into their tiny part, although she was not as bad as the one who said loudly during rehearsals for some rather deep piece of drama: "Michael, dear boy, you do realise you were abused as a child, don't you?"

It is best to deal with your director even before the first rehearsal. The simplest way is to arrive for the reading with a phoney domestic crisis that can be activated whenever necessary ("I should like to play, but you do know that my wife's ill, don't you? It might mean missing one or two rehearsals").

Ill-health is an excellent excuse because it gives one a chance to play for sympathy and to enlist the natural hostility of any cast towards its director ("He actually forced Fred to come to an extra rehearsal when the poor chap hasn't been well for months. He's just a bastard – I'll never be in one of his shows again").

For the record I shall formulate all this as the Second Wheeze of Coarse Acting: "Upon being cast, a Coarse Actor immediately suffers from illness and domestic or business crisis."

At some stage of the rehearsal period a Coarse Actor will be expected to know the lines. The length to which they will go to avoid learning them is incredible. I acted with one man who pasted a crib inside his soup plate during a banquet scene but disaster struck when he got served with pea soup instead of consomme and couldn't read it.

I have already recounted the story of the man who wrote his lines on playing cards. Starched cuffs are another good repository and in emergency cues can be written on the wrist with a ball-point pen. In costume drama I have known lines written on the blade of a cardboard spear.

If this is done, make sure you keep possession of the spear. It would be a disaster to find yourself on stage with a blank spear, or worse one with somebody else's lines.

A useful device in connection with lines is Askew's Sneer Chart. This is simply a script marked not only with moves but with every emotion and facial expression he may be called upon to register. Thus a simple line like: "You unutterable swine – you'll suffer for this" is marked as follows: "You (*breathe heavily twice*) unutterable swine (*snarl and march downstage*) – you'll (*pause five seconds*) suffer for this" (*raise right arm to 45 degrees, assume expression no. 6 and hold till curtain*).

It is also wise, during the rehearsal period, to copy out any letters, scrolls, etc., one has to read. It is rather alarming to rely on reading a letter and pull out a blank sheet of paper from the envelope.

And so the scene is set for the first night. It would seem the battle is over, but far from it. You may know things about what is going to happen on stage that the director does not know. I shall describe these in the next chapter.

3

A Coarse Actor Prepares

"Nor do not saw the air too much with your hand, thus..." Hamlet

**How to be conspicuous – conceal intentions from director –
the actor who exploded – more Unpleasantness
– when Lady Macbeth put her foot in it
– the uneasiness of Cardinal Pandulph**

Let us assume that a Coarse Actor has survived the difficult rehearsal period. The first night of the play has now arrived. What is a Coarse Actor's first thought? Surely it is: HOW CAN I MAKE MYSELF CONSPICUOUS?

Now in fact that is *every* actor's thought, the serious ones as well as the Coarse variety, but those who obtain large parts don't have to go out of their way to do it. Only the Coarse Actor, thrust to the back of a spear-wielding mob, or reduced to carrying in a tray full of drinks, has to invent stratagems and ways and means of ensuring that his friends and relatives in the audience can register his effectiveness.

In this connection it is worth quoting the experience of a friend who was playing one of a huge crowd of citizens in a play about the French Revolution. It was her first part with the company, and my friend spent hours preparing and invited all her family only to find the crowd was so dense and the stage so small, she couldn't get on stage. "There were about ten of us fighting in the wings to get on," she recalls. "I never got nearer than the stage manager's desk." A warning of the dangers of being too modest.

No, an amateur performance is not teamwork, it is a free-for-all among a dozen egos, and the ego which gets there firstest with the mostest will win.

But how, comes the question, can I get there firstest with the mostest when I have only three lines at the back of the crowd?

Well, there are certain wheezes which will achieve the desired end, and other little hints which can at least ensure that you go through the show with the minimum of inconvenience. The first is to look conspicuous.

Askew's cousin Watkins had merely to walk across the stage as a bystander in a street scene. When he went on there was such a stir in the audience I thought he must have made a rude sign at the stalls (not even a Coarse Actor would stoop as low as that for effect, although I have known a harassed comedian do it).

When I peered from the wings I saw why. He had strapped up one leg and was walking with a crutch. His face was hideous. But the master-touch was his back. He had stuffed a bowler hat up his coat to represent a hump and lurched his way across stage bent double.

Directors do not take kindly to this sort of thing, so it cannot be too strongly emphasised: no hint must be given before the first night. Many a promising Coarse Actor has had his tricks frustrated because he was foolish enough to introduce them at the dress rehearsal. The golden rule at the dress rehearsal is to lie low and go through the normal business. In Watkins's case he walked across the stage normally at dress rehearsal and then smuggled in his crutches on the first night.

The director, by the way, kicked up an awful fuss and took away his crutches, so, next night Watkins was towed in on a little trolley like Porgy in the Gershwin musical. For some reason we never saw the director again after that, but he still writes to us from Canada.

Perhaps the example I have quoted is rather a bold one, but there is certainly no reason why a Coarse Actor should not use every cosmetic aid he can find.

I shall never forget making up for my first part at The Questors, in London, as a young man just up from Birmingham and anxious to do well. I was playing Second Citizen of Angiers in *King John* and sitting next to the First Citizen. He suddenly turned to me and said, "Would you like to borrow one of my warts?"

I looked in amazement and there in front of him was a tin labelled WARTS, SCABS and BOILS from which he was liberally helping himself. Not only did he plaster his face with them, he stuck cotton wool inside his mouth to alter his features and added a huge beak made from nose putty. Finally, he rolled up pellets of damp paper into balls and stuffed them in his tights to represent varicose veins.

"You have to be pretty old to be First Citizen of an important place like Angiers,' he said. "Are you sure you wouldn't like even a scab?"

His efforts were undoubtedly rewarded because I don't think anybody in the audience looked at anyone except the First Citizen as he rose over the battlements to parley. Unfortunately, one night he sneezed and all his warts flew into the auditorium, while the cotton wool blew out of his mouth and his whole face collapsed in a shower of bits and pieces.

After the show he went round the stalls collecting any warts he could find and looking for his nose. "They take a long time to make," he said. "I've spent years building up this collection."

It was an experience I never forgot. In Coarse Acting there is no compromise. One is young or senile, fit or crippled. The younger an actor, the more decrepit he tries to be.

Incidentally, be careful of the man with cheap substitutes for cosmetics, the sort of person who says, "You don't want to use that expensive removal cream, old boy, why don't you go to the hardware store and get a tin of lawnmower grease? It's just as good and much cheaper."

After your face has burst into flames you will return to removal cream.

Of course, many shows these days are produced without make-up, especially those in intimate venues such as fringe theatres. But Coarse Actors always adapt to theatrical changes. They simply use other methods and concentrate on the physical, perhaps a tic, jerk or spasm. But if the mouth is distorted, remember to twist it downstage so it's visible to the audience.

The decline in the use of make-up has deprived the coarse actor of his greatest joys. I remember the glee in a character part of raiding the make-up box for grey hair and liners. The sad thing is that so many young actors were under the pathetic impression that they really looked old on stage. Looking at pictures of my old shows I realise I merely looked like a young man with a false moustache and lines painted all over his face.

PREPARATION. I do not hold with the school of thought which says that an actor should put himself through a series of relaxing exercises before taking the stage – a sort of yoga performance. I saw a young drama student do this. He lay down on three chairs in the dressing-room and began breathing deeply. First he raised one arm and then the other, and then one leg and then the other, until all four limbs were off the ground, and then he let them all fall with a thump. At the same time he exhaled with a ghastly hiss, like when a football is punctured. He was so wrapped up that he missed his cue.

Personally I find a quart of beer wonderfully relaxing for the vocal chords, and takes one's mind off the play. But there are obvious risks involved in drinking large quantities before going on.

Once a character urgently whispered to me, "I can't wait any longer, just say my line for me, will you, old man?" and rushed off stage. This was particularly difficult, because I was supposed to be dead by the time his line arrived.

It is especially embarrassing if you have to share a toilet with the public as in some halls and fringe venues. I shall never forget the look on the face of one of the audience when I rushed into the gents, hurled my spear and shield into a corner, and tore down my knitted chain-mail. I had an arrow sticking out of my back ready for the next scene and he kept staring at it.

A Coarse Actor is perfectly entitled to ignore any director who objects to drinking in the dressing-room. Perhaps I may be allowed to quote the exact dialogue which took place between myself and a new director a few years back.

DIRECTOR *(entering dressing-room)* Michael, is that beer you're drinking?

ME Yes, do you want some?

DIRECTOR You'd better put it away at once. It won't improve your performance you know.

ME _____

Exit outraged new DIRECTOR.

I flatter myself Coward could not have bettered the terseness of that dialogue.

But strong drink should not be taken on stage. The last time I saw this rule broken a fountain of lager sprayed from the flies on to the actors below. It came from the god in Giraudoux's *Amphitryon 38.* Finding the heat and the boredom intolerable as he waited in the flies to be lowered on a cardboard cloud, he stored some beer inside the cloud and helped himself whenever he felt inclined, which was pretty often. When it became clear bottled beer shot forth as foam at that temperature, he tried a small flask of brandy, with the result that on the last night the cloud was lowered and no god appeared. Someone peered inside and found him asleep.

Care should also be taken in what one eats before a performance.

It is unpleasant to play a love scene with someone who has just eaten garlic, cheese sandwiches or a Vampire Killer pizza. This happened to Watkins, who up to then had quite enjoyed the scene, so much so the director had to restrain him in rehearsal.

He was supposed to be positively squeaking with desire for this woman. In fact he was saying that if she wouldn't let him sleep with her he would shoot himself. The effect was rather spoiled because there was an expression of utter revulsion on his face as he spoke his impassioned words. When it came to the final clinch he couldn't face her, and just pecked the side of her neck.

Diet can cause other hazards, too. I remember a performance of a play in which a sick member of an expedition decides to shoot himself to avoid being a burden to the others. When the other explorers had left the stage ("God, but the insects are terrible, Fanshaw") he painfully crawled from the sleeping bag to the tent pole and reached up for his revolver, which was hung there. Unfortunately, as he grasped the fatal weapon he loudly broke wind. This rather spoiled the dramatic effect of his death, especially as someone in the stalls whispered, "When the stage directions said he shot himself there must have been a misprint..."

The moment before taking the stage is a particularly nerve-racking time. The best way of spending the last few moments is to make a check on costume and hand props.

A simple routine might go like this:

> Trousers – are they done up?
> Cigarette case?
> Shoes – have you got them on?
> Are your knickers falling down?
> Sword? (Ah, ha, you lent it to the French Herald, didn't you? What are you going to do now?)
> Do you know where the prompt is?
> Is the pistol loaded?
> Have you got the letter? And make sure it is not the one the stage manager gave you, but your own copy with the lines written inside.
> Do you know your way around the stage?
> (Not such a silly question. I have seen Lady Macbeth come magnificently down a staircase only to put her foot in a brazier at the bottom.)
> Do the doors open inwards or outwards?
> Have you taken off your cycle clips?
> Has anyone played a practical joke?

The last item is most important. Those who are not experienced actors may think it unnecessary, but any Coarse Actor worth his salt will agree it is vital. I shall not forget the occasion when an unpopular actor's cloak was fixed to a nail in the floor as he stood waiting in the wings, lost to everything except his part.

The man was playing Cardinal Pandulph in *King John* and the whole affair was especially interesting, because the Cardinal's entrance followed what is one of Shakespeare's worst lines: "Here comes the Holy Legate of the Pope."

Well, the Holy Legate strode on firmly, came to a sudden halt, clutched his neck with a strangled cry and vanished into the wings. The audience thought it was a brilliant piece of acting.

Meanwhile, off stage there was the sound of swearing and quarrelling and noise of a cloak being torn free. Finally the Cardinal appeared again to the accompaniment of rending cloth, and immediately forgot his first line.

All the foregoing instructions having been carried out, a Coarse Actor is now ready to make his or her entrance upon the stage. In the next chapter I shall describe how to make the best of yourself when you get there.

Incidentally, the reference above to one of Shakespeare's less-inspired lines suggests it might be interesting to hold a competition for the most banal line in classic theatre. My own choice would be from Chekhov's *Uncle Vanya*, where Telyeghin has to say the awe-inspiring words: "There's been a big fall in the temperature of the samovar." Try getting a laugh on a line like that.

4

A Coarse Actor Performs

"On the stage he was natural, simple, affecting, 'twas only that,
when he was off, he was acting." Goldsmith

Remarkable interpretation of ghost in *Hamlet* – critics dumbfounded
– how to steal a scene without saying a word – standing out in a
crowd – more Unpleasantness
– some simple wheezes

A Coarse Actor's performance problems begin *before* his entrance. How often has one watched and stared fascinated at the bulging curtains, or the wobbling scenery, which mark where a Coarse Actor is trying to grope his way on stage. For a successful performance, therefore, make sure of the entrances. Check the stage management have not nailed up the door or pinned together the curtains. They seem to have a compulsion to do that sort of thing.

Do not worry if the entrance goes wrong. Actors are most vulnerable at this point. It is at the entrance that Green's Syndrome is liable to strike. This is a desperate feeling of panic and unreality as you march into the lights. It all seems so unreal – the lights, the heat, the people. I keep asking "What am I doing here?" It is then I wish I had either had that extra gin or not had it, as the case may be.

Some actors trip up over anything within six feet. Short-sighted players, not allowed to wear their glasses, may blink owlishly all over the stage before fixing a glassy stare on the person to whom they are supposed to be speaking, unless, as often happens, they address the wrong character.

This sort of thing is less important than appearing at the wrong time – possibly in the wrong scene or even in the wrong play, as happened to Askew at a one-act festival. Don't close the door until you are absolutely sure the entrance has been made at the right point. If the cast pay no attention to you or break off abruptly in the middle of conversation it may be wiser to go out.

Make sure the cast are dressed in the same period as yourself. Askew's blunder was particularly bad because the scene was the bar of a golf club and suddenly Askew marched in dressed in a swimming costume.

Naturally, a bad entrance is rather distressing after one's appearance has been built up in preceding scenes, but fortunately Coarse Actors are not likely to have a part which is big enough for that.

A possible exception is a musical, where Coarse Actors may find themselves with a "funny" non-singing part, the entrance to which is heavily telegraphed by lines like these (to be said in a strangulated tenor voice):

Ah, here comes Rudolpho, our comic servant. He is a risible fellow and will amuse us for a moment or so. But soft, I will play a jest upon him. He will be drunk, and if I put on the Burgomaster's hat he will think that I am the old Burgher himself, ha, ha, ha.

ALL Ha, ha, ha.

SONG "The Burgomaster's Hat"

However, since it would defy Chaplin himself to raise a laugh after a build-up like that, it won't matter if the entrance goes wrong.

While it is depressing to come on stage when the situation calls for a roar of laughter, and to be received in silence, the person who has read this book will at least be prepared for the silence. He will not be left stranded in the doorway waiting for non-existent mirth to die down.

It is much worse to come on as a serious character and be received with a howl of amusement. I even had the terrible experience of being greeted with laughter as the ghost in *Hamlet*.

Admittedly I was only a teenager at the time and it was a youth production.

The director was a little worried about my interpretation in rehearsal. She kept saying, "Michael, I don't think the ghost would walk with both arms held out in front of him and wailing like that." And she absolutely forbade me to rattle some chains as I walked.

So I cut the wailing and the chains but secretly prepared what I thought would be a most effective piece of business and put it into operation on the first night. When the cue came ("See where it comes again") I held my hand out in a clutching position and slowly advanced my arm round the edge of the scenery before following it with my body. Young and foolish as I was, I thought this would be dramatic. I had not realised the audience would collapse in hysterics. The director collapsed too, I believe, but not from laughter.

All this presumes one is entering alone, but Coarse Actors frequently enter in a crowd. There is a simple rule to make yourself noticed in a crowd entrance and that is *to come in late* (the Tertiary Wheeze). The inexperienced player will try to force his way to the front of the queue in the wings, but the old hand will merely stand back, and then calmly stroll on stage about one and two-fifths seconds after the rest. It is a trick that never fails.

Incidentally, members of the chorus of amateur musicals might like to try the experiment of finishing a song a note after everyone else. It is equally effective.

Once the entrance has been made, one's duty is clear: to shine.

Remember that as a Coarse Actor you are fighting the hostility of the author, who gave the part only four lines, and bad ones at that; the director, who wants to hide you; and the rest of the cast, who have their own problems. So it will be a struggle, but a rewarding one, to impose your own personality.

You will already, of course, have found out from the seating plan the position of friends and relatives, or alternatively the critic of the local paper. Firstly, then, no matter to whom you are supposed to be speaking address key lines directly to these seats.

The effect on them will be quite remarkable, and the effect on the play will be no worse than if you were speaking to the other actors.

In this connection one must protest at the increasing tendency to produce plays in the round. How can one deliver lines to a particular section of the audience when some may be sitting behind and some in front? Askew tried revolving as he spoke and became tangled up in a telephone wire.

Furthermore, the cast are mercilessly exposed to the audience. On a proscenium stage, if an actress discovers her dress gaping open at the back she simply faces front. If an actor comes on stage with his trousers undone he can kneel behind a sofa and repair the omission. No such chance in the round. There is no hiding place.

In small theatres the audience can even read anything that is written. My friend Askew had a habit of doodling vulgar words when he had to write anything on stage and was horrified to hear the voice of a child on the front row spelling one of them out as he was taking a telephone message.

But to return to the Coarse Actor's problems. I have said that the first duty of every Coarse Actor is to project himself and I would draw the attention of earnest students to the picture, which is a classic example of how to steal a scene without having any words to say. (See photograph section: How to steal a scene, though unconscious.)

The photograph was taken during a performance of my production of *Bulldog Drummond* ("I have seldom been less in sympathy with a production," wrote the critic of that well-known literary journal the *Middlesex County Times*).

The situation is as follows: Drummond (foreground, in plus-fours) has been bound hand and foot and tied to a chair. His girlfriend Phyllis has been doped and placed in the next chair. Dr Lakington (a sadistic German scientist, in a white coat) has ordered some champagne to drink a toast before raping the girl. The champagne is brought by a Chinese mute (don't ask me why). After he brings it, Dr L. orders him from the room.

Now here is a little test. Given that situation, which actor should be able to dominate the scene?

The answer at first sight would appear to be the Chinese mute. Fantastics always steal the scene, as do children and animals. When they are mute and carrying a champagne bottle it is too easy. Drummond and Phyllis, unconscious, appear to be out of the fight.

In this production the mute made every effort to live up to the opportunity, although he was up against some severe competition from Dr Lakington, who wrote in a lot of his own lines such as *"Donner und Blitzen"* and "Chinese scum". But the mute simply grinned and winked and made vague yammering noises. He seemed a certain winner. *Yet Drummond stole the scene.*

The picture explains why. With masterly presence of mind, just as the mute was about to make his funny face, Drummond regained consciousness and started to writhe wildly in his chair, voiding himself of dreadful moaning noises. The audience immediately switched their attention to him, and the mute's efforts went for nothing.

Note that Drummond had the presence of mind to save all this for the first night. There was no hint of it in rehearsal, so there was no opportunity for me to cut the business (which I most certainly would have done). I do not approve of anyone getting a laugh in my productions unless I have the credit.

CROWDS. It is possible for a skilled actor to stand out even in a crowd, despite the handicap of having no lines. Here is an example from a production of *Julius Caesar*.

Watkins was in the crowd, playing nothing particular, just one of the rude mechanicals – Sixth Citizen, I think. He was not considered good enough to have any lines, not even gems like "O woeful day" which the first, second, third, fourth and fifth citizens were spouting.

Yet he overcame this handicap in an extraordinarily simple manner. During Mark Antony's speech over the body of Caesar he carefully placed himself centre stage and simply repeated every other line that Mark Antony said, illustrating the words with gestures.

The scene eventually went something like this:

MARK ANTONY Friends, Romans and countrymen, lend me your ears...

SIXTH CITIZEN Ah, ears, ears, ears. *(Nodding and grimacing to the other* CITIZENS*)*

MARK ANTONY I come to bury Caesar, not to praise him.

SIXTH CITIZEN To bury Caesar, not to praise him. *(Making vigorous digging motions)*

MARK ANTONY The evil that men do lives after them. The good is oft interrèd with their bones.

SIXTH CITIZEN Their bones, their bones. *(Holding up fingers)*

When Antony came to the lines: "Here is the will and under Caesar's seal. To every Roman citizen he gives, to every several man, seventy-five drachmas", Watkins danced for joy and began to count imaginary money. Every time Brutus was mentioned he spat.

In fairness to Watkins he was only adopting a traditional technique much loved by bad film directors, where the standard crowd noise is to repeat the last line of what the main character has said. One can hardly blame a mere amateur for copying the device.

In addition to the above, crowd members are traditionally licensed to write in vague noises of their own invention, grunts such as Urgh, Aaah and Yurch, plus the inevitable Hooray-ray-ray: all-purpose coarse cheering sound. At the end of any rousing speech a crowd may gain extra lines by announcing what they intend to do. Examples are: "To the Bastille!"; "Death to the traitors!"; "To the breach, to the breach!"; "On towards Dunsinane!"; "Arrest Peer Gynt!"; etc., etc. So as to make no mistake, Askew actually prepares his own script for crowd scenes, a sheet of paper covered in ejaculations and grunts. He also believes the traditional crowd noises should be in period. Thus in *Julius Caesar* he was distinctly heard to mutter "Rhubarbum, rhubarbum..."

As stated earlier, it is a tradition of the Coarse stage that members of a crowd will be maimed and crippled, and will gibber meaninglessly. This applies not only to the Elizabethan period, but right up to about 1880. From then on crowds are deemed to be less deformed. It is also customary that at the start of a scene two cripples painfully limp from opposite sides of the stage, cross and resume identical positions the other side.

Another tradition is that on entering everybody greets each other as if they've not met for a long time. The greeting, for some reason, usually consists of a punch. Some years ago at the National Theatre I saw a crowd scene which looked more like a prize fight, and that wasn't even Shakespeare, it was Galsworthy's *Strife*. They went on swiping at each other for hours.

And a final point: whenever a part of the human body is mentioned, point to it. It's a rule ingrained in the Coarse theatre. "Lend me your ears," is an obvious example. This doesn't only apply to crowds. Even leading roles have a tendency to clutch their chests when "heart" is mentioned. In opera it's compulsory.

But even among crowds there is a code. If anyone tries to hog the scene too much, the others are perfectly entitled to sabotage his efforts. The best way of doing this is for everyone to gang up on offenders and stand in front of them. They cannot do much behind a wall of living flesh.

TECHNIQUE. The amount of genuine acting which a Coarse player will be called upon to do is limited. To start with he will merely be called upon to register certain simple emotions. The only emotions that need be used are as follows:

1. RAGE   4. JOY
2. PLEASURE   5. PAIN
3. LOVE   6. HATE

And even in this simple list the same expression may serve for two emotions. (See pictures) Once a player is able to register these stock emotions successfully he can introduce subtleties by mixing two emotions.

Have no truck with any director who requires impossible subtleties of feeling. If he says "I want you to give me that underlying sense of insecurity" simply hand him the list and ask him to tick off the required emotion.

STAGE FIGHTS. A skilled actor can make a piece of wood seem like a sword. A Coarse Actor can make a sword seem like a piece of wood. The pattern of a Coarse sword fight is traditional. Grunting is substituted for sword-play and both contestants spend much time circling round apparently trying to grunt each other to death. It helps if they grunt on different notes, otherwise it becomes monotonous. The actual circling is done with bent knees in a kind of waddle. Under no circumstances should the sword be pointed at the opponent. It is always held with a slight slope backwards, towards one's own side. That way there's no danger of anyone getting hurt. (*Or of the fight looking realistic.*)

If action is called for, blows are aimed at the opponent's weapon and never at the person. Usually this is done to pattern: clash swords at shoulder level, clash at knee height, clash again at shoulder level in a figure eight motion. Sometimes one swordsman is out of time and the other has to wait, or even prompt the other as to what to do. Actors have been seen to mouth "Stab me" at their opposite number.

But by far the best way of fighting is simply to lock hilts (*or shields*) and rock to and fro, grunting. This gives the actor a chance to rest and look round the audience for his mother or girlfriend. Occasionally a daring director will allow a character to beat his opponent's shield with his sword but Coarse actors are usually so scared they don't hold their shields over their bodies but raise them high in the air so the opponent has to jump up and down to hit them.

Another variation is for an actor to swipe at the legs of his opponent, who escapes by jumping over the sword. Not advisable. Usually the actor jumps too soon and has landed before the blow is struck or else he jumps too late with fatal results. Indeed, last time I saw that happen the offended swordsman lost his temper and the fight started in earnest and was carried on in the wings, where shouts and cries of pain punctuated the next scene.

Most sword fights end in death. The usual way of simulating this is the traditional Royal Shakespeare Armpit Death. The loser holds out one arm, a sword is passed under the armpit, and he lowers the arm trapping it. His opponent then makes great play of pulling out the sword *(it is best to avoid putting a foot on your opponent's stomach)* and the loser dies horribly.

A simple alternative is for both actors to lock hilts or shields and for one of them to drop dead suddenly. There is a third death, in which the fight moves off-stage, there is a cry of pain in the wings, and the winner returns with red toothpaste all over him. Coarse Actors should favour Method Three – it is less dangerous.

As you value your life, never allow a fencing expert near rehearsals. I shall never forget a college production in which the fencing champion played a part. The audience cowered in their seats as his sword whirled flashing arcs over the edge of the stage. Most of the actors cowered too. His opponent didn't even put up a fight. He shrank into a corner waiting to be killed.

And after hours of rehearsal practising ripostes it will all revert to normal and people will be slain by jabs in the most unlikely places. I have seen at least two productions where people were killed by a sword thrust in the buttocks.

Askew once had to kill a rather violent actor who loathed him. The wretched man not only refused to die but attacked Askew with such violence he fled from the stage, bleeding at the forehead.

The difficulty now was to have the man slain, since Askew refused to return until he was dead. Finally the stage manager succeeded in hissing from the wings "Die" and he took the hint.

The same technique should be applied to fist fights as to sword fights. Never mind the director, just go into a harmless clinch and grunt. Don't believe any maniac who says no blow hurts if you ride it. I have seen this theory tried out in rehearsal and it took half an hour to bring the man round.

If you have the misfortune to play a part which requires you to be struck on the head with a club insist on personally inspecting the weapon before the performance. Some property mistresses will provide a club like a young railway sleeper. It is, of course, possible to make a hollow club with a tongue of wood on a spring inside which will give out a realistic sound at the slightest tap. If props have provided one like this I have only this piece of advice:

Throw it away, preferably in the direction of the person who made it.

Alternatively, try it out on the head of the director. These things invariably go wrong and deliver a stunning blow. In fact the safest thing is to make your own club out of string, cloth and old newspaper. It won't sound very realistic, but you'll survive.

Test all dangerous business on the director. Pretend not to understand what he requires and ask him to demonstrate.

"I'm sorry, Ron, I don't quite understand how I ride the blow when he pushes the broken bottle in my face... I wonder if you'd just show me."

It's surprising how quickly these things are dropped when that technique is adopted.

DEATH. Coarse death, like sword-fighting, is traditional. No matter where the wound is, the pain is always felt in the bowels. You'd think if someone had just died the Royal Shakespeare Armpit Death they'd cry, "My God! My armpit!" and clutch the wounded place but no, they just hold their bowels like all the others. I remember a production of *Julius Caesar* in London and Caesar was stabbed six times in the back by the senators and each time he held his stomach. The symptoms of poisoning, stabbing, shooting and bludgeoning are all similar – the victim should seize the bowels firmly and sink down with a gurgle. Habit is so strong I've seen someone do it when strangled.

In this connection I always think of President Reagan, who suffered many wounds in the real Coarse manner as a Hollywood actor, yet when a would-be assassin shot the poor chap in real life he simply fell down, as millions saw on TV. An example of the difference between the stage and reality.

Be sure to die in a comfortable position. Ignore any director who wants an actor to hang around for half a scene draped over a grandfather clock or some such nonsense. My advice to the aspiring body is to die behind something and then have a good sleep. If one is in view there is always the danger of heavy breathing or even a sneeze, apart from the strain of having to lie still (see photographs, ways of dying).

Dying gives great opportunity for a Coarse Actor. It is not often realised that on the stage dying people speak louder than the living and at greater length (just look at those Shakespeare death speeches or any opera). It's also interesting that villains tend to die noisily and heroes silently. Hamlet just peters out in Horatio's arms but King John expires raving and ranting. Indeed, I played with one King John who extended his death by regaining consciousness just as they were carrying him off and started to groan again. The audience could hear this dreadful gurgling passing into the wings and then becoming fainter as it moved to the dressing-room, where it finally ceased as he went into the toilet.

Have nothing to do with sadistic directors who want death with blood all over the stage, directors who expect an actor to go through a scene with a bladder of blood hidden in his bosom or lie by the footlights with a sword sticking vertically out of his stomach. This may well result in the Unpleasantness which occurred to Askew's cousin Watkins, whose blood-container developed a leak long before he was due to die, so he appeared to have a haemorrhage in the middle of his dinner.

Finally a little advice on the curtain call.

My first words are simply never take one. To start with, the curtain is an embarrassment, being the worst-organised part of the show, rehearsed for the first time at about eleven o'clock the previous night. At the best the curtain will either stick or rise for a hastily milked third call to reveal everyone tiptoeing off or making rude signs at the audience.

At the worst there will be one of these clever calls in which everyone tramps round in a procession until the audience are exhausted with clapping, so those coming on last enter to silence.

Apart from anything else, a curtain call may make the cast late for the boozer.

However, if you have the misfortune to have to take a curtain at least use the opportunity to draw attention to yourself. One method, especially suitable for women, is to pass a hand across the brow, totter feebly, regain composure with an obvious effort, and collapse as the curtain comes to. This has the added advantage of cutting the ground from under the feet of critics. Obviously you were under strain the whole evening.

More unusual, but quite effective, is to break ranks, march to the leading man and shake him warmly by the hand (or kiss the leading lady). No one will know why you have done this but the audience will think you must be important.*

---

* This may seem incredible, but I once played with a man who was in such a hurry to get home he used to put on bicycle clips for the curtain call.

5

Be Prepared

"And in the next-door room is heard the tramp And 'rhubarb, rhubarb' as the crowd rehearse..." John Betjeman (Summoned by Bells)

Trapped on stage – the pistol which wouldn't – how not to give a prompt – the Unpleasantness at Northampton – collapse of elderly theatre

The most important thing a Coarse Actor can master is a knowledge of some common crises which are liable to arise on stage. By anticipating a crisis he can often come out of the situation with an advantage over more talented players. There is no question as to whether a crisis will arise. Law Three of Coarse Acting states: "Every production will be accompanied by a crisis." It is a sign of inexperience to believe a show can go on without a hitch.

How often does one hear an actor say in rehearsal something like: "I know one night you're going to drop that blasted vase." Yet how many actors trouble to prepare for the inevitable dropping? Directors would be much better advised to spend time rehearsing what to do when something goes wrong than in discussing obscure points of interpretation.

DOORS AND EXITS. Doors are troublesome objects. *(Law 4: "Scenery doors are not designed to close or to open")* There is little that can be done about the door which slowly swings open during a scene unless one gets up and shuts it, in which case it will almost certainly swing open again. Good for a laugh, but not much else, especially if someone has just cried out, "We're trapped, I tell you." I do not advise the stage manager to reach a hand round and pull it shut unless she is at loggerheads with the director and wishes to gain revenge by spoiling the show.

Worse, however, is the door that won't open, so an actor can't get on, and, even worse, the door that won't let anyone off, so you wander desperately around looking for a way of escape. In the first part I ever played (as a schoolboy in *Goodbye, Mr Chips* at the old Leicester Theatre Royal) I even tried to go out of a door that was painted on a flat. I must have looked stupid clawing at the canvas with my nails; Mr Chips, who was supposed to be dying, had to get up and show me the way out.

Never force a door. Have you ever seen an entire box set slowly teeter inwards and bury Lady Windermere? If you have then you will not viciously tug at a door that refuses to budge.

If a door will not open the best thing to do is to look for another exit. It is usually possible to squeeze out somewhere, or even through the audience.

Do not escape through the fireplace as this is unrealistic.*

Should no other exit be available the stranded actor must let the rest of the cast know of his predicament. Have a line ready in keeping with the play. For a comedy one might say, "The old door has jammed", but in a thriller it would be more appropriate to bellow, "My God they've nailed up our only way of escape!"

PISTOLS, ETC. Stage pistols and firearms do not work.

This is not stated as opinion but fact. A special type of pistol is issued, which fires one shot in ten. It is safer to presume a pistol will not go off, or if one is fired off-stage that will not work either. So have a spare death.

My friend Askew, after uselessly clicking his revolver half-a-dozen times, suddenly leaped on the astonished victim and finished him off with a knife from the sideboard. As he did so there was a loud bang from the wings where the stage manager had got the emergency gun to work. This was rather different from the Unpleasantness at Leeds, where legend says the killer ran up to his victim and kicked him when the gun failed. With immense presence of mind the victim shouted, "You filthy rat! The toe of your boot was poisoned!" and dropped dead.

---

* Unless playing Father Christmas

It is a good idea for killer and victim to get together and decide who is to say the emergency words. What must be avoided is for *both* of them to say the emergency lines, so the victim totters around crying, "The whisky had cyanide in it, you scum," while the murderer is shouting, "Another victim for my silent automatic."

Fortunately, most murder weapons are not as unreliable as pistols. There's not much that can go wrong with a dagger for instance. Or is there? Some years ago there was a production of *Macbeth* where as Macbeth picked up the daggers to murder Duncan the blades fell off. Lady Macbeth, thinking she was saving the situation, swept across stage magnificently and cried:

Infirm of purpose!
Give me the handles!

I suspect she was one of those people who would come off-stage afterwards and say, "Believe me, the audience never noticed a thing."

CRÊPE HAIR. Never trust to luck. "I think it'll be all right," is the stage equivalent of "The cheque's in the post." It only needs the vapour from a cup of tea to start a moustache or beard working loose. Spirit gum should be included in the stage manager's kit, for an emergency repair in the wings. Askew claims an SM once re-fixed his moustache during a scene in which he spent some time leaning out of a stage window.

COLLAPSE OF SET. A Coarse production rarely passes without some sort of trouble with scenery, whether it's a curtain ripped down or the collapse of an entire wall. So, as with firearms, be ready. Teetering flats may be supported by an actor or actress leaning against them; it is important for the rest of the cast to co-operate and take over when the time comes for the supporting actor to make an exit. Sometimes this is impossible, of course, and I recall an Othello who had to strangle Desdemona from long-range while holding up a tottering pillar.

In *Coarse Acting Two* at the Edinburgh Fringe, someone blundered into a doorpost in *The Cherry Sisters* (a Chekhov spoof) and the whole set threatened to fall. It was saved by the cast, who propped it up until the interval. Genuine mistakes in a Coarse Acting Show are not usually funny, so we were relieved when a local radio station commented that the swaying scenery "was inspired comic invention." But don't rely on being so lucky.

It is, however, a law of Coarse Theatre that scenery which is *meant* to collapse will never do so. It is all very well for R.C. Sherriff to write in the stage directions for *Journey's End:*

> *The shelling has risen to a great fury. The solitary candle burns with a steady flame, and Raleigh lies in the shadows. The whine of a shell rises to a shriek and bursts on the dugout roof. The shock stabs out the candle flame; the timber-props of the door cave slowly in, sandbags fall and block the passage to the open air...*

But that is exactly what will not happen on the night.

In a Coarse production the wretched dugout will collapse in the first scene without a shot being fired, and then obstinately refuse to show even the smallest sign of weakness at the end, when it ought to cave in.

One of the saddest things I have ever experienced in a play was to see Watkins screaming in the middle of the stage: "Mercy... mercy...the whole house is falling about my ears..."

At this point the ceiling was supposed to collapse. He was still repeating the line minutes later while teams of stage hands sweated with jammed ropes and pulleys.

Eventually they brought the curtain down, and the ceiling promptly fell on the heads of the cast while they were taking the curtain call.

UNEXPECTED APPEARANCE OF STRANGE CHARACTERS. Be prepared for people to appear on stage who are not supposed to be in that scene. They may wander about trying to say lines and can become abusive until they realise their error, which should be pointed out by another actor in a whisper. Do not try to attract their attention from the wings or they will stare off-stage scratching their heads, or else give a hoarse cry of alarm.

Even more alarming is for people to appear on the stage who are not in the show, a hazard to which performances in public halls are particularly vulnerable. A policeman once marched on-stage in a London suburb and demanded to know who owned a car which was blocking the entrance. The play stopped immediately, since the owner was one of the actresses. Another time I was at a village hall when a doctor wandered through the scenery into the middle of a murder mystery. Someone in the audience had fainted and they'd phoned for him and he'd come in the back way. On this occasion, though, the cast tried to continue, but the doctor became irritated at being ignored and asked to see the patient in a commanding voice.

It was then that the actor playing the detective committed one of the bravest deeds I have seen in the theatre. Realising the doctor must be got rid of at all costs he stepped forward and boomed, "I think you have a lot of explaining to do, Doctor – or should I call you Major Fairfax?" With which, he dragged the wretched medic into the wings and handed him over to the stage manager.

CHARACTER FAILING TO APPEAR. Don't waste time gagging. Go off stage and fetch him. He will probably be found gossiping in the wings or playing cards in the dressing-room.

Warning: An actor in Birmingham was watching from the wings when there was a hiatus on stage. Realising someone had failed to make an appearance he ran to the dressing-room to fetch him, when he discovered the missing person was himself.

Even worse than someone not appearing on stage is when they fail to reach the theatre at all. Ways in which players prevent themselves from reaching the theatre in time are incredibly ingenious and there should be a prize for the best. A sure winner would be the man in Edinburgh who fell asleep one afternoon. Meanwhile his flatmate, who was also in the play, thinking the flat was empty, went out, locked the mortice lock on the front door, and vanished with the only set of keys. The actor awoke to find himself locked in an hour before the curtain rose...

The scene now changes to the theatre where a panic-stricken stage manager was confronted by a strange woman, holding a grubby piece of paper.

"Someone threw this out of a third-floor window in Bruntsfield," she said, "and shouted for me to take it to St Paul's Church Hall. Does it mean anything to you?"

The SM took it. The message simply read, "For God's sake tell Harry to come and let me out."

INTERFERENCE FROM AUDIENCE. The smallness of theatres and halls makes Coarse Acting especially prone to this hazard. The interference can range from the evil schoolboy who grabs the bottom of a cloak to the old dear who puts her teacup on stage. Not to mention the child who recognises his parent and bleats loudly, "Why is that man sticking that sword into my daddy?"

Included among hazards must be the case of the talkative front row who are not above addressing the actors directly. It is most disconcerting to come on stage and hear a voice say loudly, "Here comes that man you don't like, Mum."

Just as bad was the lady who once leant forward from the front row and said, "You've dropped your glasses." I knew I had dropped them, it was a subtle part of the plot which nobody was supposed to notice, and here was this idiot booming it all over the auditorium.

Audiences also feel that they have *carte blanche* to express their disapproval publicly. In one Bond play we used to play a game of guessing who had walked out.

"That's the Chief Constable," Askew would whisper to me as there was the sound of a seat being violently tipped up and a disturbance in the audience. Someone else would say no, it was Councillor Frogworthy, he always walked out when sex was discussed.

The strangest interruption from the audience that I can recall came because of a prop. Someone lent us a violin. It looked merely a broken-down old fiddle and we treated it roughly. On the third night, during a scene where two people wrestled for possession of the instrument, one of the actors had the brilliant idea of hitting the other on the head with the violin. It broke.

Immediately a wail arose from out front and a formidable woman stood up.

"How dare you treat my violin like that," she boomed. "Do you understand that it is over fifty years old?"

Well, we tried to carry on as if nothing was happening, while everyone cried "Sssh", but the woman would not stop.

"Look at you," she shouted, "you've not even said you're sorry. And now you've put it on that chair where someone will sit on it." (That was the whole idea.)

At the interval she marched backstage and demanded the return of the violin. This was unfortunate because it had a key part in the next act, but she insisted and we went through the rest of play with a violin hastily constructed from a piece of broom handle and some cardboard.

CLOUD OF STEAM ENTERING AUDITORIUM. An unusual crisis, but experienced at more than one hall. It is caused when the refreshment tea is being made near a door into the auditorium. Two minutes from the interval the door will open, a cloud of steam will obscure the audience and a female voice will boom: "Is it the interval yet?"

The odd thing is that however much the timing of a show changes, the steam-laden apparition will appear at the same spot each night, almost as if she had a cue for it. As it is impossible to compete with a cloud of vapour, there is nothing that can be done except to keep calm.

Do not answer the question about the interval.

BLACKOUT FAILING TO HAPPEN. One of the worst stage horrors is when a blackout fails to come, leaving the cast stranded on stage. I shall never forget a play about the Russian Revolution in which the crowd were hanging a priest. The unhappy priest stood at a platform with the rope around his neck and the crowd leader pulled a dummy lever on stage, which was supposed to open a trap underneath the priest. Simultaneously there was a blackout, which covered the fact the priest was still there. End of scene. Applause.

Alas one evening the blackout never came and the priest was left standing on the platform in full view. For a moment he just stood there and then desperately tried to save the situation by uttering ghastly choking noises and attempting to claw the rope from his throat. The executioner lost his head and kept pulling his lever again and again while we in the crowd invented face saving dialogue such as, "We had the same trouble last week when they hanged the capitalist" and "It worked better if you don't open the trap" and similar rubbish.

The blackout fell at last on a devastated production.

CURTAIN FALLING IN MIDDLE OF SCENE. This is quite likely to occur if there is a line similar to the curtain line. It is best not to take up the curtain immediately, as this would indicate that the whole thing was a mistake. Instead, wait for about half a minute, and the audience may think it was a genuine break. An actor on stage when this happens should control himself and not indicate surprise or dismay when the curtain starts to come to. Under no circumstances try to hold it back physically.

The converse of this disaster is for the curtain to rise unexpectedly, or more frequently for a blackout to end too soon. It is best simply to assume all blackouts will end before the cast are settled and then one is prepared for the worst. Once again the curse of acting in the round is well illustrated by the unfortunate experience of Askew's sister Maureen, who failed to get off stage in an exit blackout and found herself alone in the acting area when the lights went up, with people trying to sell her chocolate.

INTERVAL COMING IN WRONG PLACE. An unusual hazard, but one I have experienced at a fringe theatre. It was an experimental work by an unknown author, and consisted largely of blackouts and grunts. The house manager mistook one of the blackouts for the interval and immediately switched on the house lights and started marching up and down the aisles offering ice cream. Meanwhile the actors were in full swing again. The poor author stood up in the auditorium and bellowed that it was all a mistake, how could the morons eat while his play was going on, etc. etc., but nobody paid any attention.

SHOWER OF SALIVA DRENCHING CAST. It's a paradox of the stage that often the best actors shower everyone with spit. The bad ones don't articulate well enough to do so. I well remember being extensively gobbed over by Anthony Quayle when I sat in the stalls at Stratford during his triumphant Lear, but I regarded that as a privilege. With someone less talented (such as Askew) it is not such a blessing. The answer lies with the director who must encourage the offender to face front, or indeed anywhere except opposite his fellow-actors. The audience may suffer but they are only there for one evening; the cast have to endure a whole run. Make certain you know where the spitter is facing. If spat over on-stage do not flinch; turn aside or bury the face in the hands, overcome with emotion.

FORGETTING LINES. It is important to remember it is no use to rely on the prompter, even if there is one, which is by no means certain. However, if there is a prompter the first duty of any Coarse Actor is to ascertain his/her position, so that in case of emergency one can work to the prompt side and whisper, "Yes m'dear", out of the corner of the mouth.

In this respect it helps to keep in character. For instance, in an Elizabethan play one could mutter, "Yea coz?" so the audience might think it part of the play.*

Remember that a clumsy march across the stage is worse than useless. The essence of the operation is to move firmly yet subtly. If possible try to find some business for taking you right across the stage. Perhaps the director could help by having a small drinks table placed on the prompt side.

Of course, whatever one does is no use if the prompt is half-witted. On one of the many occasions I have dried, the voice of the prompter, a keen young girl with spectacles, rang out loud and clear. It was such a change to have an audible prompt I nearly applauded, only what she said was not much use. She simply said:

"And."

Well, that wasn't enough, so I sidled off towards her and when near enough hissed, "And what?"

"And the..." came the reply.

In the end I had to go off-stage and seize the book.

Prompters are usually female but the worst I ever met was a man. New to the stage, he didn't really know what he was there for and when people dried he said nothing except "Wrong";

---

* Don't blame me if you get the reply, "And yea coz to you, mate."

if the actor struggled on he would say, "Still wrong...getting better...nearly right."

If you are sufficiently *en rapport* with another member of the cast you might have an agreement that he learns your lines as well as his own, while you do the same favour for him. This is not such a strange suggestion as it sounds, because one of the symptons of a Coarse Actor is that he always knows other people's lines better than his own.

The late Kenneth More once told how he saved a colleague from disaster by knowing both sets of lines. The poor fellow was playing a jailer, come to tell More details of his execution. Alas, he opened the cell door and dried completely, so More got the dialogue from him by question and answer:

"I expect you have come to tell me the details of my execution?"

"Er...yes..."

"There is a rumour going round the dungeons that the rack has been specially strengthened."

"Er...yes..."

"It will be a horrible death, will it not?"

"Er...yes..."

"And afterwards I shall be hung up for the birds to eat?"

"Probably..."

"And buried in unconsecrated ground?"

"Definitely..."

But this is a technique only for the experienced.

In opera and musical shows, drying is less of a problem because the audience frequently can't hear the words anyway. If stuck, one can usually get away with a sort of meaningless groaning, an all-purpose Coarse lyric noise which comes out like, "Hooly hong, I hah hee, ace eeh harch..." When the chorus come in, try to pick up the gist of the song from them. As a last resort simply sing "I love you," repeatedly. It fits most duets. Alternatively, the conductor might give the line if looked at appealingly.

In extreme cases of amnesia, it might be possible for a kindly member of the stage staff to follow a player round the set whispering prompts from behind the scenery. A girl did this for me once when I had to take a role at short notice; her voice floated mysteriously from behind cupboards, underneath sofas and even from inside a gas stove. I always feel sorry she married somebody else as she obviously has a very resourceful brain.

Askew is one of the few people I know who has actually taken a prompt from the audience. Apparently there was someone in the front row who knew the play (or at least knew it better than he did, which would not have been difficult) and he was astonished to hear his line floating up from the stalls. His astonishment, however, did not prevent him from accepting the prompt with gratitude. Whenever he dries, he still glances at the stalls, just in case...

Beware of the evil-minded actor who forgets their own lines and manages to throw the blame on the person opposite. This can be done in several ways, for instance by asking a question that's not in the script. A veteran pro I knew, one of the old school who knew Shakespeare backwards, actually made up a stock speech in blank verse to get out of trouble when he dried. If he forgot the line in a Shakespeare play he would stare the actor opposite in the eye firmly and say:

> Thou weariest me.
> Unto my chamber shall I now retire
> And rest me on my couch a little hour.
> Farewell, until we meet again, farewell.

With which he would sweep off-stage, and watch his victim try to deal with the situation. We all came to fear the sudden blank look on his face which showed he'd dried, followed by the dreaded "Thou weariest me..."

Some directors work on the theory that if there is no prompt then nobody will dry.

Never take part in any such production.

I hang my head in shame at the Unpleasantness in Northampton when we were playing *The Servant of Two Masters* in the open-air without a prompt. Not only did we do it without a prompt but without half of the second act one night, thanks to myself and the man playing opposite. We are still trying to decide who was to blame.

PLAY GOING ROUND IN CIRCLES. Another common danger. It occurs when a character has similar lines at different parts in the play and saying the second line triggers off an automatic response in another actor who says the reply from the earlier part and the whole thing starts again. Watkins swears he saw a production in which someone tore off their false beard and immediately there came a line similar to one earlier, they all went back ten minutes, and the man had to replace his beard.

AMNESIA. Forgetting who you are is not uncommon. At least twice I have entered and said something like, "My liege, I am –", or "Good morning, my name is –" and suddenly realised I've forgotten who the hell I'm supposed to be. So always write the character's name on your wrist. This will also avoid the unpleasantness which occurs when you're playing several parts and you introduce yourself by the wrong name.

COLLAPSE OF THEATRE. Not a frequent occurrence except in areas subject to earthquakes, although I can remember a great chunk of plaster bursting like a bomb in the audience. The sight, however, of half the audience evacuating their seats owing to a leak in the roof is by no means unknown. Above all, keep calm and do not hold out a hand to see if it is raining. Askew claims that a theatre really did collapse about him a few years ago. He was playing in a large marquee which fell down in the third act, burying actors and audience alike.

MEGALOMANIA OF KINGS. I have been a servant to seven English monarchs, cupbearer to the King of Denmark, messenger to the rulers of France and Bohemia, bodyguard to the Queen of Egypt and close attendant upon the Doge of Venice. All upon the stage, of course. I've been stabbed by kings (once when it wasn't in the script), hanged by kings, tortured by kings, rewarded by kings and in *Richard III* something quite unmentionable happened to me. But it's what happens off-stage that I wish to warn about. Believe me, wearing the cardboard crown has no small effect on these monarchs of the outer suburbs, which is quite understandable when you consider that for a rehearsal period of maybe seven weeks they spend nearly every evening condemning people to death and kicking grovelling messengers around, or in the case of queens, being wooed by six monarchs at once.

The king's attitude begins to harden during rehearsals. There is a tendency to ask courtiers and clowns to fetch props or run errands. But the megalomania bursts forth completely at dress rehearsal when he stands twitching neurotically in the dressing-room, surrounded by attendants changing the royal armour, doing up the royal surcoat, carrying rude messages to the stage manager and returning with even ruder ones. On the first night the king can bear no one near him, except for an occasional slave to fetch aspirins and brandy. To disobey is unthinkable – the habits of rehearsal are too strong.

Worry not. The king's reign is short. On the last night rebellion will rear its head, and the kings sense it. They start trying to be friendly and offer to buy drinks. Now, if the king has over-played his hand he is liable to be subjected to pranks. The cider in the royal cup may be replaced with ink, or part of the crown removed. The game is up. Tonight dies royal Richard, tomorrow he becomes Mr Smith of Sidcup who is rather interested in amateur theatre. Watching a stage king return to reality always reminds me of that quotation about Charles I, "...saddest of all kings, crowned and again discrowned..." There is something to be said for being a Coarse Actor after all. The return to reality is so much less shattering.

RATIONING OF VITAL EQUIPMENT. There's never enough of anything to go round in Coarse Theatre. I have played in a production with two swords and three shields between ten soldiers; and another with one musket among five. Not to mention when two top hats had to be shared between eight men and one radio mic between a whole cast. The way to deal with this is to have a chart pasted up off-stage showing the destination of the vital prop, together with notes like, "Harry carries off top-hat and passes it to maid who brings it on to give to John on exit." The maid was written in; she kept coming on and handing people hats. This chart was presided over by a female dragon who exerted the strictest discipline. Do not rely on the cast looking after themselves as players will never do anything with a prop except take it to the dressing-room and lose it.

Even so, one English soldier could find only a French shield, complete with large fleur-de-lys, for the battle. He'd invited his mother to see the play and she said afterwards, "What were you doing in the wrong army, dear? Were you supposed to be a spy?"

6

The Director

*"The notes taken by the director as he silently watches the players
are a test of his competence. If, for example, he writes: 'The Oedipus
Complex must be very apparent here. Discuss with the Queen',
the sooner he is packed out of the theatre and
replaced the better" Bernard Shaw*

**Lack of talent no bar – Unpleasantness in London – a howl in
the night – don't bother about the author – when to be horrid
to the cast – the Diary of a Disaster**

Far from being in charge of a show as the title suggests, the
director is at everyone's mercy. His (or her) magnificent creation,
product of months of thought and rehearsal, can be destroyed in
performance by the smallest bit-part player or a schoolgirl ASM.
And there's nothing they can do. They cannot force people to act,
they can't rush on stage and tell somebody to stop waving their
arms about or to speak up; they are helpless when the blackout
never comes or the whisky runs out or the table collapses.

Fascist stage managers may ban them from backstage and
everybody will blame them for failure, especially the cast. Indeed,
I can't think why anyone should want to direct if they can act.
Yet there is a queue of people waiting to do so. I've even done
it myself. I think it's the eternal hope that next time you'll get
it right that keeps one going.

Lack of talent is no bar to becoming a successful director.
Modesty is the greatest handicap. It is not necessary to know
anything about drama or the theatre, but it is absolutely essential
to give the impression of knowing everything.

The sort of talk which never impresses an amateur group is the good old plain man-o'-the-boards stuff ("Quite honestly, I reckon a director's first duty is to get 'em out of each other's way and make 'em speak up.") Anything practical and down-to-earth like that dooms a director from the start.

It is preferred, even in the lower strata of the dramatic world, if one talks in vague phrases that mean nothing. For example, one might say: "Believe me, I am not interested in the mere mechanics of speech. It is immaterial whether the audience hear my actors speaking, but it is absolutely essential that they should hear them *thinking*."

Having been chosen, however, a Coarse director must set about casting the play. It is essential to have a reading for parts. This, of course, will be completely disregarded as a basis of casting, which has already been done over pints of bitter and cups of coffee elsewhere, but justice must appear to be done. If anyone should complain, the director can always say, "I didn't like your reading, ducky."

But a word of warning. Shun the casting couch.

Any director who would cast a woman merely because he has hopes of her favours is simply a human rat, devoid of morals. Not only that, but you stand a much better chance of success with women if you don't cast them. Once their object is achieved by being cast, their attitude changes rapidly and they will produce an incredibly good-looking young man at rehearsals, with whom it appears they have been madly in love for years.

Although the casting couch should be eschewed, there is no need to forego the casting pint. I kept myself in free drinks one winter by dropping hints to people that they looked just right for the lead in my next show. Actually, I wasn't directing anything at all, but they kept buying me drinks.

Sometimes, directors don't have a free hand in casting. In many places certain parts are in the gift of certain people, like rectorships in rural parishes. Even tiny servant roles may be the prerogative of wizened little men who help with the lighting when Fred's ill. As to whether these local traditions are followed depends on whether you wish to direct there again.

IMPORTANT WARNING: Never cast your wife or husband in your own show.

However, let us assume the casting of the play is complete. The director must now consider his approach to the whole thing. If he is wise he will adopt one rule in dealing with a Coarse cast – be as simple as possible.

With sorrow and sadistic pleasure I recall the fine directors reduced to gibbering madness by the built-in obstinacy of companies and back-stage staffs. I remember years ago directing for the Women's Institute.

I wanted a woman who was supposed to have just received a shattering shock to give a ghastly, inhuman wail off stage. I wanted the cry of a soul in anguish, the half-human sob of a woman at the end of her tether.

I don't think we rehearsed anything for six weeks except that blasted sob. The first time she did it, it sounded as if someone was being sick in the wings. At other rehearsals she simply stood there and bellowed like a cow in pain. In the end I said we had better cut the sob, and she went all sullen and said she was just getting it, and it was helping her feel the part.

On the first night I carefully left the Memorial Hall before the sob came, and went for a drink. I was just about to enter the bar when from the hall came an indescribable shriek which froze my hand on the door and echoed through the silent village night. The shriek was followed by a chorus of barks and bellows from every farm for miles around.

The landlord asked me anxiously if I'd heard that ghastly sound outside and I confessed I'd not only heard, I was partly responsible for it. He thought I was joking.

Once I read John Bourne's excellent book *Teach Yourself Amateur Acting*. I read it on the advice of a director who drew me gently aside and said: "Michael, I want to recommend you a book on acting. Please promise me you'll read it, dear boy. It might help you to stop waving your arms about."

Mr Bourne quoted as an example of inventive business the scene in *They Came to a City* where Joe sits and talks and smokes. Mr Bourne suggests that he should roll his own cigarette instead of merely lighting one.

Now this is just what a director must avoid. It's bad enough when a Coarse Actor has merely to light a cigarette – the trembling hand, the match which won't strike, the frantic puffing at a dead cigarette – but to roll one would be a disaster. This doesn't only apply to Coarse Actors. Since smoking became a capital offence (well, almost) and the cast are non-smokers, they often find cigarettes a problem on-stage. They can't even light a fag and if they do, turn green after three puffs and look for somewhere to stub it out (which they also don't know how to do).

It's a far cry from the days when veterans used cigarettes as an extra finger, an extension of their nicotine-stained hand, while actressess welcomed the cigarette holder, which gave them an air of sophistication. Offstage, too, cigs might be stubbed out on the inside of a shield before entrance; sometimes people's faces burst into flames as crêpe hair caught fire. Indeed, one of the rules of Coarse Acting was "Always hand your cigarette to the stage manager before entering". This was one of those little disciplines which distinguish a true gentleman of the boards.

The most a director can hope for from his cast is that they will get on stage somewhere around the cue, say their lines more or less accurately, or if not their own lines, someone else's, and then exit without knocking over the scenery. Instructions should therefore be kept as simple as possible. It is no use asking for the sound of a man in spiritual torment. At least, you can ask for it, but you won't get it. What you will receive might be recorded for use as a fog signal, but that's about all.

Clever business tends to dominate rehearsals to the exclusion of the play. Two hours are spent on Jane's conjuring trick; five minutes on her big speech. I shall never forget a man, who fancied himself as avant garde, directing for a rather twee group. There was an 18th Century crowd scene and wanting to show the sordidness of life then, he asked one of the men to pretend to urinate against a wall. It took over the whole play. Several of the cast protested; every rehearsal was interrupted with long debates. The original urinator eventually went on strike ("How can I be expected to have a piss in front of my aunt?") and was replaced by a suspiciously keen volunteer who destroyed the scene on the first night by what can only be described as disgusting over-acting. Details on request.

Directions to the cast should be reduced to the following:

SPEAK LOUDER	SPEAK SOFTER
SPEAK SLOWER	SPEAK QUICKER
MOVE LEFT	MOVE RIGHT
MOVE DOWNSTAGE	MOVE UPSTAGE

And the average Coarse Actor has difficulty even in grasping those. If no directions at all are given it can generally be assumed that they will mumble unintelligibly and mask someone.

A director will usually find all his energies are taken up with the sheer mechanics of keeping some sort of order among the cast and getting through the rehearsals. It will help him to do this if he remembers the techniques which it is possible to use.

A. The Ingratiating Technique: "Now that was wonderful, boys and girls, absolutely wonderful. Sheila dear, I must say I was a teeny-weeny bit surprised when you sat down for your big speech... Yes, dear, I know you were tired, but you see it's more effective standing up... No, no, no, I'm not criticising you, darling, honestly I thought the delivery was just terrific. Possibly a deaf person sitting at the back of the hall might not have heard every single syllable, hmmmm?..."

B. Hail-fellow-well-met Technique: "Right, gather round, everybody. Bert, hand me that bottle of beer, will you? Now listen, darlings, that was all right. Fine. OK. We've got a production here, we've definitely got a show, boys and girls. Honestly I laughed my head off. Fred, that bit of business when you fell flat on your face was just fine...fine. But don't overdo it, mate. Cut that idea of getting your head stuck in the wedding cake. You old ham *(punching him)*, you're just an old scene-stealer. No, I love it..."

C. The Doomsday Snarl: "God, that was pitiful. Slow, no energy, no concentration. You do realise you'll have to do it before an audience in 144 hours and six minutes, don't you? And some of you don't even know the lines...yes, Anne, I know you've had problems...yes, I do know divorce isn't funny... OK

Harry, so they made you redundant...we've all got troubles...
Right, we've got thirteen and a half hours of rehearsal left to
get it right so let's get cracking this time..."

Professionals guesting with amateur companies are much
inclined to favour the Doomsday Snarl, perhaps because they've
invited all their friends from the BBC to see the show. They
never seem to come.

In an effort to impress, a director is perfectly entitled to
mangle an author's script as much as he likes. Anyone in the
publishing business will confirm that authors are lower than
dirt, anyway. Just for guidance, the order of seniority in a play
goes as follows:

> Person who puts up the money
>
> *Professionals only.*
> Lighting or wardrobe departments
> Set designers and constructors
> Stage management
> Treasurer of the Company
> Leading actors
> The director
> Coarse Actors
> Theatre cat
> The author

The very pinnacles of the stage have set the example of
wrecking an author's work, from the time when Colley Cibber
started pepping up Shakespeare (among other things he added
the line "Off with his head" in *Richard III*). Of course, if he
had been a modern director he would have changed the locale
to Italy as well.

Only recently I played in one of those what's-the-use-it's-
all-hopeless types of plays, written by an aspiring local author,
which ended in utter misery, like this:

ALF It's all a rotten, stinking cheat. That's all life is. A dirty
    word. It takes your youth and your hopes and your dreams,
    shatters them and leaves you a prisoner in a sick, ageing
    body to drag out the remains of a weary existence until

you die horribly in a seedy lodging-house. Oh God, how I hate myself.

Enter GERT, *his girlfriend.*

GERT Alf?

ALF Get out, you stupid bitch.

He sobs uncontrollably, She screams and rushes off. There is a sound of a shot offstage. ALF *lifts his head, pulls a bottle of sleeping tablets from his pocket and starts to stuff them into his mouth as the curtain falls.*

The DIRECTOR *rewrote this to read:*

ALF Sometimes I wonder what life is all about. If only there was some hope somewhere.

Enter GERT.

GERT Alf?

ALF Gert...you've come back... I knew you would, darling. Together we can face the future...

They stand looking at each other tenderly as the curtain falls.

As I was only playing a bus-conductor I didn't mind, but the poor author was almost deranged. Nobody had the courtesy to tell him of the alterations, so the first he knew about them was at the opening night, when he interrupted the curtain by coming on stage and taking a swing at the leading man. Then he persuaded his agents to send us a stream of rude letters and writs and injunctions. Not that it did any good. The well-established rule of TV, radio and the stage is that the last person to know anything about a work of art is the person who writes it.

Occasionally lines really do need altering, but for some reason directors will never amend the lines which genuinely need attention. Askew and I used to go into fits every night at the rehearsals of a play which contained the lines:

"Has the Doctor seen her, Fanny?"

"Yes, and he said there was little hope."

The actress who said the first line invariably omitted the comma, but the director saw nothing wrong. He simply put on a twisted smile and said he didn't think everyone had peculiar minds like ours. The result was that on the first night the show stopped at that point with the audience in tears of mirth.

A further act of rewriting that may be needed is to amend the play to accommodate fifty extra people. This especially applies to musicals. In societies with more acting members than there are parts to go round, it is often customary to squeeze in the surplus at all costs, even if it means amending whole chunks of the play. A longstanding friend tells how when he was in *The Desert Song* at Leeds he was astonished when twenty extra Arabs – mostly women – wandered on stage for the second verse of one of his numbers. "They were literally coming out of the rocks," he told me. The extras then sang the rest of the song with him (despite the fact it was supposed to be a solo) and disappeared into the rocks again.

I remember a production of *My Fair Lady* in which a complete dream sequence was written in. While Eliza sat in Professor Higgins's room all her old Cockney friends passed by the window, one by one, singing and leering at her. As this society had an enormous acting membership the procession took about half an hour. I'm sure some went round twice.

Having mutilated the play to your satisfaction, it may now be blocked. As an author's lines are fair game, so are his situations. After all, one must ensure the audience know some sort of direction has gone into the thing.

The classics, in particular, are easy meat for a nice spot of mutilation and as these days it does not seem to matter how the verse is spoken there is endless opportunity for showing how superior the director is to the unfortunate author. In any case, accessibility is today's buzz-word and a director is expected to popularise classics.

Part of a typical mangled production of *Macbeth* might well go something like this:

Enter **MACBETH**. *He is dressed in tennis kit. He prowls round the stage eating an apple.*

MACBETH If—

He throws the apple core out of the window.

Itwurdunwentisduntwere

WELL

A raven is heard croaking.

Twere done.

He turns an hour-glass upside down.

Quickly if the assassination could

A dog walks across the stage. He kicks it. There is a long pause while he roams around belching.

Trammel up hmmm?

A-a-h the consequence and catch

A distant bell chimes.

WITH HIS SURCEASE! ! ! !

A bag of soot falls on his head.

Successssss. *(in a tiny whisper, a cannon goes off)*

Fortunately, the poor quality of most Coarse Actors means a director need not worry himself too much about this sort of thing. Moves and business should be kept as simple as possible. An audience will have much more fun from unrehearsed crises, such as when the sofa collapses.

At some point a person calling themselves the set designer will appear. Have nothing to do with them. Whatever conception the director has of the play, the designer somehow takes a different view.

Some years ago I played in a production of *Lear* in which the director said he considered Lear was a man trapped in a tube; the designer saw him lost in a symbolic wilderness. They never did get together. The director gave us all tiny movements with Lear huddled up in corners like a foetus; the designer burst forth with a great open stage, relieved only by a vast phallic symbol in the middle.

A wise director is prepared for this. He or she takes the stage manager into their confidence and rehearses with the set as they would like it. However, if you consider Lear is stuck in a tube I suppose such devices are above you.

Most Coarse Actors have little idea of their whereabouts on stage so a director may have trouble with masking. There is a simple way of avoiding this. Do not tell the offending person to move, as they will merely shuffle in front of someone else. Simply say to the player being masked, "Betty, Fred is masking you." Betty will immediately remedy the situation herself.

A Coarse cast is also very gregarious. Unless watched they always huddle in groups on stage or else get in a ghastly straight line.

At an early stage in the rehearsal period a director should make a careful note of all psychotics in the cast and weed them out. This is probably the most important task. Psychotics include gripers, moaners, weirdies and people who are always being ill.

Some of this type can be spotted at once, such as the man who misses the first rehearsal with an excuse about having had a fainting fit. Unless checked immediately he will appear spasmodically then vanish altogether a week before the opening night. Have him out at once.

Watkins played with one chap who vanished for a fortnight just before the show and then had the cheek to turn up on the first night after somebody else had been called in to replace him. They had a great row in the dressing-room, both of them fighting to get into the same costume.

I would include know-alls among psychotics. If any person comes to a director after the first reading and starts offering advice and comment – have him out. This sort of person causes endless trouble in rehearsal, holding everyone up for hours to discuss futile points of interpretation of one word. In the dressing-room he advises everyone on what to do and then comes on without a vital prop.

Another important task early in rehearsal is for the director to pave the way for his disappearance, in case the problems are too much. He or she should quietly drop hints about a possible business trip abroad ("My God, I hope they don't send me to Sweden just when I'm getting to grips with the production..."). This excuse can be activated when you can't face any more.

As rehearsals progress the difficulty will arise of the cast's slowness to learn lines. A simple way of encouraging them is to threaten to cut any speech that is not known. By some miracle the actor usually learns the speech in the next ten minutes.

But be careful if you have any of the Method school in the cast. I knew an earnest young disciple who had one line in a play. They cut this at the first rehearsal, but every time we came to that spot a spasm used to flit over his face.

When asked what the trouble was he replied, "I've got the thought, but not the line." In the end they had to put the line back.

A further problem for the director is that all actors love being maimed and wounded. I have already told how Coarse armies limp.

I was in *Oh, What a Lovely War* once and cast in the scene where the wounded soldiers arrive at Waterloo. The first rehearsal will live long in my mind as the injuries grew and grew. "Please may I be blind?" we all chorused at the director. Those who weren't allowed to be blind were jealous and compensated by asking, "Would it be a good idea if I had one leg/arm? I sort of feel I've been wounded in the groin...can I have a crutch?" By the end of rehearsal the room was filled with limping, hobbling, bandaged, gibbering wrecks, hanging on to each other and falling down at every chance.

Female Coarse Actors usually have the opposite syndrome. They insist on being beautiful whatever the occasion. You see them in *Mother Courage* carefully arranging their hair in the dressing-room to look pretty and then putting one little black smudge on their cheek to show they are meant to be sordid.

Rehearsals up to the dress rehearsal will be mostly a waste of time, except for helping cast to learn lines and moves. All that is achieved by any rehearsal not on stage is to train the cast in wrong ways, e.g. going out of exits which do not exist, or where the sideboard will be.

Whatever takes place at the dress rehearsal will bear no relation to what has gone before. The first thing discovered is that the set is completely different from the plan used in rehearsal. Probably the designer has omitted a door, so all exits and entrances are impossible.

Even if the set does have the requisite number of doors it is probable one of them will open on to a brick wall. One might think this would only happen with a hired hall, but in fact it is just as likely to occur in a theatre, which the designer has known for years. Sets are not designed for acting in, but as exercises in artistry.

The set will not fit the stage. Law Five states: "All Coarse Acting sets are designed to be six inches bigger than the maximum possible size."

The furniture will be at least four times as big as that used in rehearsal. Property mistresses must scour the junk shops of the world for elephantine pieces. Usually, when all furniture and props are set there is no room for anything else (and that includes the cast).

Anything other than speaking or squeezing between the furniture will be found impossible. The drink of whisky which was so important cannot be managed because to reach the sideboard it is necessary to climb over the sofa, which in turn is blocking the door through which the man who drinks the whisky has to enter. The fight scene has to be cut.

To make matters worse, the rehearsal will have to continue with men and women in overalls crawling like flies around the stage. I do not know why it is, but set painters, electricians, sound engineers and so forth do nothing while rehearsals are going on and then suddenly spring to life just as the dress rehearsal starts.

Also, all sorts of strange people who normally are never seen crawl out of little holes and make their presence felt. I was present at one dress rehearsal where a man started to mend the roof with a hammer just as the curtain rose.

Forget the old tag about a bad dress rehearsal preceding a good first night. A bad dress rehearsal usually means a bad first night – and a bad second night, come to that. In fact at the dress rehearsal the Coarse director is face to face with the stark truth.

Tell the cast just how bad they are without mincing words. Besides, this will be the last chance to give them a torrent of abuse, so let them have it for all it's worth. Don't worry about depressing the cast – a depressed cast is a good cast, especially in comedies. The amount of laughter from the audience is usually in inverse ratio to the enjoyment of the cast. Ideally they should be nervous, sweating, depressed and worn-out.

This will effectively stop any tendency to laughter and giggling on stage, and if a director can achieve that with Coarse Actors he has certainly accomplished something.

Incidentally, don't let the cast see a programme at the dress rehearsal. The misspelt names and grammatical and factual errors will merely infuriate them.

Although one may insult actors and actresses as much as one likes, never be vituperative to stage staff. They go sullen and threaten to strike. I know, I've done back-stage work myself, and I don't know a more touchy and slow-moving scene-shifter. One can't help it – a strange sense of resentment creeps over you.

Eventually the first night will arrive. The director's final job before the curtain goes up is to make sure all the cast are present and if necessary arrange for substitutes to stand by. He himself will already have learned a smattering of everyone's part.

This routine must be kept up right to the final performance. I remember a production of my own in which I sat happily watching the last night. All my troubles seemed over and I was almost enjoying it for once when there was an uneasy pause. I dashed back stage to find that one of the actors hadn't turned up. While the cast fluffed their way through we telephoned his home.

"I thought the show finished last night," he explained plaintively. Seizing a copy of the script, the stage manager and I there and then rewrote the play to cut out every one of his subsequent entrances. But somehow the rest of the show seemed to lack something. It was also a traumatic experience for an actress who was on stage the whole time. There was no way of telling her what had happened so she looked on in bewilderment as whole episodes vanished, lines were said by the wrong people and the man in love with her never appeared.

A Coarse director can never count himself at ease until the curtain has fallen on the final performance, and even then there may be some unpleasant legacy to deal with, such as the ruining of the costumes or the fact the society tried to dodge paying royalties.

Don't forget to have a word with the stage manager before the curtain rises. My publishers will not allow me to print the word, but have it all the same.

Some directors spend the performance backstage, interfering with the cast and stage staff and throwing everything into confusion. The first time I met one of this type was a severe shock. I was in the middle of a speech when a rasping voice from the wings ground out "Pep it up, old man" and I turned to see the angry face of the director peering at me over the prompt's shoulder. It completely unnerved me.

I don't, however, suggest a director should sit in the auditorium all through the show. The strain would be too great. Personally I always go over to the pub as soon as the first actor dries. This means I am in there by about seven-fifty-five. Return at the first interval, and it is surprising how much better the show will look.

Never go on stage for a curtain call, even if called for by the audience. People will only say it was all rigged. Besides, immediately the curtain has fallen it is your duty to seek out the representative of the local Press and ply them with drink.

Then go backstage and congratulate the cast. Don't tell the truth. Thank them. Then go home. Avoid the last-night party. Drink loosens tongues and aggrieved actors and actresses may be unpleasant, not to mention the stage manager.

And if the day has been a bad one comfort yourself as you crawl into bed with the unfortunate experience of a man who was once directing Dame Edith Evans. After rehearsal had been on for half an hour, during which he had made several ineffectual interruptions, she turned, fixed her eyes on him and said loudly, "Who is this person?"

At least nobody has been *that* crushing.

APPENDIX TO CHAPTER SIX

Suggested timetable for an amateur production taking place on April 1:

Jan. 1 – Feb. 1: Cast play secretly.

Feb. 3: Formal reading for parts. Results ignored.

Feb. 7: Production conference. Discover designer plans to do whole thing with a Z-shaped stage.

Feb. 8: Resignation of set designer.

Feb. 10: Anonymous insulting phone call received. Believed to emanate from aggrieved actor.

Feb. 12: Set designer calls at home and drinks all the gin. Very penitent.

Now wants to do play on L-shaped stage.

Feb. 13: Designer resigns for second time.

Feb. 14: Insulting Valentine, with obscene overtones, received from unknown source.

Feb. 15: First read-through. Half cast absent. Copies of play apparently not available in Europe.

Feb. 16: Blocking rehearsal. Cancelled after half an hour as no one knows what the set will look like.

Feb. 17: Three characters drop out.

Feb. 20: New designer, wishes to perform the play on a "womb-shaped stage". Unfortunately, nobody knows what shape a womb is. Stage manager marks out a rectangle for rehearsal but is told a womb is not square.

Feb. 22: Resignation of new designer.

Feb. 24: Leading man announces he cannot attend any more rehearsals on Mondays, Wednesdays and Fridays.

Feb. 27: Approached by original set designer, who is willing to concede that play can be done on conventional stage.

March 1: Leading lady says she cannot attend rehearsals on Tuesdays, Thursdays and Sundays.

March 7: Treasurer of society says he is very worried about the amount of money being spent on set, costumes and lights. He only got to hear of it when Strand Electric rang up to ask when they wanted to take delivery of the back-projection equipment.

March 8: Rehearsals cancelled for three days for conferences with wardrobe, lighting department and designer.

March 10: Resignation of wardrobe, lighting staff and designer.

March 14: Wardrobe mistress arrives in tears and starts sewing again.

March 17: Set designer reappears as if nothing had happened.

March 19: Abusive phone call received.

March 24: Leading man drops out.

March 25: Leading man replaced.

March 26: Leading man offers to return. Refused.

March 31: Final Dress Rehearsal: Discover forestage obliterates two rows of stalls. New lighting man arrives and fuses all lights halfway through first act. Finish 1am. Home 2.45am.

April 1: First Night: Insulting message waiting at hall.

Just before curtain rises notice there is something odd about the way the chairs are arranged and discover box office are working to the original stage plan, with the result there is a Z-shaped gap in the audience.

After three minutes cast start going round in circles so leave auditorium to pace up and down outside. Buoyed up by many congratulations after show, then depressed by former leading man, who says he thought everyone *tried* hard. Overhear conversation in toilets in which two people are saying what they *really* thought of the play. Bitterly depressed. Drown sorrows.

April 4: Read local paper account. "Hard-working cast very funny situations...slick business...bore comparison with West End standards...brilliantly directed..."

April 5: Suggest to committee that might be willing to tackle another production next year, if can spare time, etc., etc.

All-purpose Coarse expression (female): hate, grief etc. Can also be used to indicate physical illness such as indigestion or approaching death.

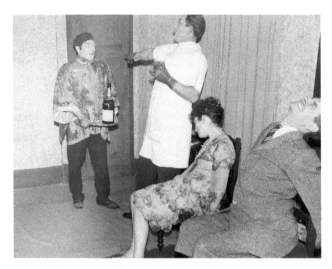

How to steal a scene, though unconscious.

Traditional way of killing: The Royal Shakespeare Armpit Death.

Wrong way to die. This pose is impossible to hold. Also the knife will slowly teeter to the floor.

Correct method of dying. All is ease and comfort.

Wrong way to take a prompt.

Basic all-purpose Coarse costume (female). Suitable for all periods in history and any part with fewer than six lines.

The author wearing all-purpose Coarse costume (male).

The man on the left has read this book.

The girl on the left has also read this book.

If your production photographs look like this, the company
qualify as Coarse actors.

A Coarse actor press-ganged into playing a Shakespearean clown.
He has obviously failed to raise a laugh, except among the cast.

Stock Coarse character number seven (sea captain). The picture shows a performance of masterly understatement.

A scene from a classic tragedy, probably Ibsen. The real tragedy is that the actor forgot to check his trousers.

An unfortunate accident in a sword fight when the action became too heated.

On the Coarse stage dying people speak louder and longer than the living.

Don't get carried away and put your foot on your opponent to draw out the sword.

What happens if you are rude to the wardrobe mistress.

This man married the wardrobe mistress.

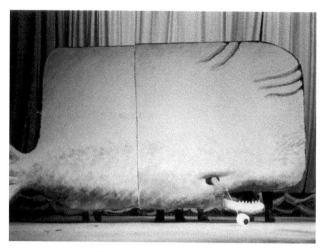

This production of *Moby Dick* was nearly spoiled when the whale's eye fell out, but an alert ASM retrieved it.

One of Shakespeare's greatest scenes, 'They won't notice it's an oven glove.'

Pity about the infant prince. He got trodden on.

7

The Open-air

"Warble his native wood notes wild..." Milton

The prompt which reached Southend – Unpleasantness on the roof of a public convenience – when Maureen sank – difficulty of playing in fog – when your crown turns to wet cardboard

Law Six of Coarse Drama states that on the performance of any play in the open-air:

1. An immense flock of screeching birds with loose bowels will fly to and fro over the audience and the stage.
2. The Air Traffic Controller at London Airports will immediately re-route seventy-five jet airliners over the acting area.
3. A karaoke contest will start in the pub across the road.
4. Five cars will crash noisily in the vicinity, with a screeching of tyres.
5. Rain, fog and tempest will descend without warning.
6. The local chapter of Hell's Angels will hold a rally nearby.

Yet despite all this there are still brave souls who like acting in the open-air, and those who like watching, and I have a soft spot for it myself, despite my criticisms.

A director in charge of such a show must first of all realise that no one in the audience is going to hear more than half of what is said. Even so, avoid the temptation to employ microphones and amplifiers.

If these are used it will be found that they are of a special type, issued only to amateur companies, which pick up nothing but the noise of the wind. While the actors are mouthing hopelessly all the audience will hear is a scratchy, booming sound, with an occasional ear-splitting electronic shriek.

The only time I knew a loudspeaker to work was when the prompt used it. She was ingeniously tucked away behind a bush, since there was nowhere else to hide her. A speaker was concealed in a tree and she was supposed to whisper any prompt into the microphone. Our electrician assured us the speaker was adjusted to be quiet yet audible to the cast.

The first prompt could have been heard at Southend (the show was in the Midlands). In fact Petruchio, who was leaning against the tree containing the speaker, leaped two feet in the air when he heard it. Worse, the microphone was so sensitive it picked up every rustle from the prompter's clothing, so the first half was punctuated by mysterious crackling noises and breathing sounds, until we rescued the poor girl at the interval.

Another of the difficulties over audibility is that more people will be watching the show from outside the auditorium, than from inside. (Law Seven of Coarse Drama: "Every open-air production is sited near a public convenience with a flat roof, which will be crammed with juvenile delinquents.")

As a child at the seaside I remember a concert party on the sands who used to send the chief comic round on an expedition to clear the children off their free perch on top of the public lavatory ("Go on, Charlie, hop round and get them kids off the urinal"). But somehow I don't see this working with an amateur group.

Fortunately, the dampening effect the open-air has on a voice works in the opposite direction, so players are blissfully ignorant of the chattering in front of them and that their speeches are vanishing around the third row. Against this, actors can see the audience. It is deeply depressing to watch people stand up and file out in the middle of a speech. Worse, there is the danger of being distracted by what is going on. I saw a woman in the front row get out a meal from a picnic hamper and slowly eat it during *Tom Jones*. When she produced a banana and painstakingly peeled it, the action on stage slowed to a standstill with the cast staring fascinated.

The Minack, in Cornwall, with its beautiful cliff-top setting, provides some wonderful experiences. I shall never forget standing on the little path behind the stage and watching three sharks swim into the bay.* But the theatre can be difficult, especially as the audience face the sea, which is often more interesting than the performance. My best moment in *Playboy of the Western World* was ruined by the appearance of a rescue helicopter and the lifeboat.

There is a praiseworthy local tradition that the show must go on, so it sometimes does so with a storm raging and props blowing out into the Atlantic, while a drenched cast struggle to pretend they are in the sitting-room of a country house. An added worry for the company is that some may be camping and have an uneasy feeling that it's not only the scenery that is being blown away, but also their little bivouac at Logan Rock.

Fog, apart from the obvious dangers, produces a special hazard there, because it triggers off coastal foghorns whose terrible blasts interrupt the play at regular intervals. One horn is timed to coincide with the length of an iambic pentameter, so Hamlet's famous soliloquy would sound like this:

To be or not to be, that is the question. (Baaaaarp)
Whether 'tis nobler in the mind to suffer (Baaaaarp)
The slings and arrows of outrageous fortune (Baaaaarp)

Yet a fog-horn is preferable to the peacocks at Abington Park, Northampton, who regularly interrupted open-air performances with their weird mating cries. Some of drama's tenderest moments were ruined by the screech of a peacock having an orgasm.

Whereas in an indoor production the setting can be adapted to fit the play, in an outdoor show the play has to be adapted to fit the setting.

---

* Unfortunately the director was not bathing at the time.

But be careful. It might seem very nice to have someone swing from the branches of a real tree like a gorilla, but in practice either the branch will break or the park-keeper will chop off the only suitable branch just before the performance.

Askew's sister Maureen had an unhappy experience while playing Ariel. The director wished to make use of a very pretty lake, which framed the acting area, and placed, a few inches under the water, a series of concrete blocks, so Ariel could appear to tiptoe over the water.

Unfortunately, a child in a paddle-boat, finding his navigational rights obstructed, moved a block to one side, with the result Maureen vanished up to her thighs in mud with a fearful screech.

That was a production which had everything a director should avoid, including a live horse, which fertilised the stage while someone was seated on it, making a speech. There was also an orchestra on a floating platform at the side of the lake. I should like to say that the platform sank, but the worst that happened was that the mooring became untied and it drifted slowly out, gradually turning round so the orchestra had their backs to the audience.

I suppose the greatest experience of the open-air theatre is the pageant or community play. There seems to be a sort of standard form of acting for pageants, in which nobody pays any attention to the principals or the plot and carries on as suits them best. A man who played in his borough history show told me that when he was Simon de Montfort addressing the serfs he noticed every single serf had their back to him. They were looking at their friends in the audience.

The impression of Coarse acting on an enormous scale is heightened by the futility of the dialogue, which is probably composed by a local butcher:

Enter a **THANE** *with an arrow in his stomach.*

SECOND THANE Art thou wounded, Olaff?

FIRST THANE Nay, 'tis but a scratch. But tell the King we must away...

An experienced open-air director will *never* make alternative arrangements to perform indoors if the weather is bad.

The mere fact of making such arrangements seems to ensure a supply of freak storms and depressions. The whole of a director's day is one long worry as he glances at the clouds every five minutes wondering whether to ring up the stage manager and tell her to put all the chairs in the hall, and finally about five o'clock, as the heavens open, he makes his decision and teams of sweating stagehands transfer the whole production into the hall or marquee.

As they are carrying in the last chair a blast of heat strikes them, sunshine of a hitherto unheard-of intensity floods the park and a rainbow glows mockingly over the deserted acting area.

Sooner or later in the show the director will be faced with the most awful decision of all. Do we go on through this downpour, or do we stop now?

I have played with the press-on-at-all-costs type who insist on continuing, with the remnants of the audience huddled under trees and peering furtively from their umbrellas, while the actors' costumes cling soggily to the skin and the cardboard spears begin to fall apart. And I have played under timid directors who call it all off at the merest hint of a shower, while the audience sit in shirtsleeves and grow restive.

Personally I would say press on. People may not appreciate the acting but they do admire the courage, and while they may not stay to see the show finish, at least they will have a word of praise for the cast when they return home ("I don't know how they stuck it in all that rain. And that poor King, with all the gold paint running off his crown...").

In fact it will probably be the only time in a Coarse Actor's life that he will receive the genuine and unstinted admiration of the audience. The fact that all the costumes will be ruined will be a small price to pay.

8

The Stage Manager and Back-stage Staff

"I'll come no more behind your scenes, David; for the silk stockings and white bosoms of your actresses excite my amorous propensities...'
Dr Johnson

Power of stage manager – stage staff need not remain unseen – how to blow up the theatre – all-purpose Coarse costume – Unpleasantness with a property club – collapse of elderly director – hideous meals

No position offers greater influence over a production than stage manager. (I use the term to include male and female.) Once a show is running, the director is helpless. But just as Coarse Actors may have an effect out of all proportion to their importance, so it needs but one dozy ASM to forget to ring a doorbell to reduce a highly dramatic scene to rubbish. Worse than forgetting the doorbell is to ring the telephone instead, leaving the cast desperately improvising. Most actors are only too well aware of this. That is why they are so friendly to the stage manager. And that is why people like being stage managers.

In theatre generally stage managers and their teams are usually spoken of as working unseen and out of the glamour of the lights. In Coarse Theatre, however, stage management are frequently far from invisible. Indeed, there are times when they appear in full view of the audience, to general delight and, I suspect, to their own satisfaction, since in every Coarse Stage Manager there is an actor trying to get out.

There was, for instance, the occasion in Ealing where the designer had the brilliant idea of cutting the set down to three pieces of mobile scenery. Each piece consisted of three flats fixed together to form a hollow triangle on tiny wheels, and in the middle of this stood an operator, hidden from the audience, wheeling the scenery about as the action demanded.

The play (the plot of which, I am afraid, rather eluded me) had many changes of scene, all taking place in Egypt some five thousand years ago. The effect was most impressive as the blind monoliths buzzed about the stage, now clustering to represent a grove of trees, now lined up to act as a city wall.

Unfortunately, one of the triangle operators was myself, and on the second night, after a triumphant opening performance, I was rather slow wheeling off at the end of a scene, and found myself stranded on stage in a blackout.

I'm afraid I panicked. The audience rustled as they saw a tall, dim shape, with one wheel squeaking slightly, rushing all over the stage in the half-light. I made one dart to where I imagined the wings to be and was rewarded by a horrified shriek from the stalls. Apparently I pulled up six inches from the edge of the stage while the front row abandoned their seats. Eventually, with all sense of direction lost, I twirled miserably centre stage hoping for something to happen.

It was then that I became aware of someone knocking on the outside of my triangle and a voice called urgently: "Mike, Mike. Are you there?"

It was the stage manager. I shouted, "Yes" in a voice that could have been heard all over the hall and he replied, "I'll get you out of this, matey."

Guiding me with a torch, he led me off stage, rather in the manner of someone helping an elderly lady through a fog, and released me from the wretched triangle.

Later we discovered that the blackout had lasted two minutes. The front row of the audience never did return.

Of course, that is only one example of a stage manager appearing to the audience. There are many others, such as the time at Northampton when a flat fell down to reveal the stage manager glued to the back of it. Apparently she had been trying to hold the two flats together by the well-known Coarse method of The Human Cleat and her weight over-balanced them.

There is no need for an SM to be ashamed of wishing to appear to the audience. He should wear a gaily-coloured (preferably fluorescent) sweater, so that if his arm has to appear round the edge of a flat, to replace a fallen prop or beckon an absent-minded actor off-stage, the audience will be in no doubt as to whose arm it is. Personally when stage-managing, I always have my initials embroidered on my arm, just in case. It is most gratifying to hear from movement in the auditorium that your arm has not only been seen but recognised.

I have, in fact, known an SM and his helpers remain on-stage for a whole scene. It happened in a production of an operatic society where they were supposed to transform the setting swiftly during a blackout. Unfortunately they were running late and the caretaker of the hall threatened to pull the plug on them at 10 o'clock whatever happened. So the conductor started up the music, the lights went up and the cast came on. Meanwhile the stage management toiled on, trying to get sofas through tiny doors and hang a huge chandelier, as *The Merry Widow* thundered on all round them. The actors won by a short head and actually finished the scene before the stage hands had finished setting it. "It's all go with this bloody lot," said the stage manager afterwards.

The true Coarse stage manager regards the mechanics of the job, such as calling actors, exerting back-stage discipline, etc., etc., as mere details, to be left to the unimaginative assistant stage managers. He or she will be more concerned with the artistic side, such as inventing a set of lies for the local authority about fire precautions, and seeing there are plenty of *empty* fire extinguishers lying about. Remember that full fire extinguishers are dangerous, as they may go off at an awkward moment.

Both in rehearsal and during the show be prepared to deal with difficult callers, for the mere fact a show is being performed seems to attract a string of strange persons to the hall. My friend Askew tells me of the time when a Water Board man was found wandering behind the scenery in *Three Sisters* and had already been glimpsed through the window, to the mystification of the audience.

It is worthwhile for a stage manager to check that the performance is taking place in the correct hall. This is the sort of precaution which an inexperienced person would not bother with, but a Coarse stage manager never trusts anyone, least of all the secretary of the company.

If you have ever had the mortification of actually starting a performance, only to find that you are entertaining the wrong body of people in the wrong place, you will understand what I mean. We thought there was something odd about the audience; in fact they were a group of pensioners expecting an old-time music-hall and they were very upset when we launched into Pinter's *The Caretaker*. "When's the sing-song going to begin then?" the old dears kept calling out. The performance was swiftly abandoned when the real entertainment arrived with apologies for being late.

SOUND EFFECTS. I sometimes feel nostalgic for the days when nearly all sound effects were produced by the stage manager in the wings. It was sheer bliss to turn the handle of the wind machine with the thunder sheet going full blast and someone madly rolling dried peas on a bass drum beside you (that's how we used to imitate a storm). Often the enjoyment went to our heads and we drowned the actors, who could be seen making desperate signals to the wings to ease off. Ambitious stage managers would add a few rolls of thunder unexpectedly in the middle of a scene. In *Henry V* the whole cast were called in to help and battle noises were simulated by banging tin plates and mugs together off-stage while everybody went "Urrgh, aaaah, blurch" etc.

I was once in a play where an ASM had to produce three effects single-handed. With one hand he turned the handle of the wind machine, with the other he pulled a cord that made curtains billow on stage, and at the same time he shouted for help, since someone was supposed to have fallen into the sea. I watched him in admiration as he flailed about every night. Sadly, his efforts brought little reward. On the first night I asked a friend in the audience what he thought of the effect, and the man said sourly, "It came over like someone turning the wind machine and flapping the curtains. And what was that man shouting in the wings?"

But electronic sound doesn't guarantee a trouble-free run. It's only as good as the operator. Not long ago I saw a herald raise a trumpet to his lips and there came forth, not a fanfare, but a recorded announcement about mobile phones. To make it worse the operator realised what had happened and cut the announcement. The herald was left soundless so he walked off. As he reached the wings the fanfare came.

At the Edinburgh Festival Fringe occurred what must be the ultimate disaster: a performance of *Krapp's Last Tape* by Beckett in which the tape failed. Since the play consists entirely of a man listening to his tape recorder, the results were catastrophic. As a cynical member of the audience called out, "Why didn't you call it Tape's Last Krapp?"

It is strange how producing sound effects brings out aggression. Sound operators must be watched stringently. Left to themselves they will obliterate any show.

I once played in a production of *Oh, What A Lovely War* in which the battle effects were in the hands of an audio-maniac, who was not content with the odd whine and crump in the background, but continually interrupted each speech with great moans, thuds, rat-a-tats and an obscure sound rather like an old bus exploding, which he said was the exact noise made by a three-inch mortar. The actors never had a chance. So don't blame me if the production is taken over by a little man in the sound-box. You have been warned.

I confess to having a personal interest in the production of stage effects, since I once wrote a book about it. It was the funniest book I have ever written and contained this gem: "To make a noise like a tray of crockery being dropped, fill a tray full of broken crockery and drop it." I only wish I could write stuff like that these days.

However, it seemed to fill a need, because several people wrote to me and said how helpful the book was. There was also a letter from a man who complained that in following my advice on how to produce a realistic air raid he set fire to the theatre.

Lovers of Coarse Theatre may be interested to know how he did it. He strictly followed instructions that maroons should be exploded in a dustbin, for safety's sake, but he forgot to tell his ASM what the dustbin was for, with the result that she filled it with wastepaper shortly before he let off the maroon. Not only was there a splendid blaze but members of the cast were showered with burning paper.

Crowd effects may be part of the stage manager's task. Remember to keep exhibitionists out of an off-stage crowd. It is better to have a few people murmuring "Rhubarb" than to have a lot of would-be actors making up strange lines of dialogue.

The people to avoid are those who regard shouting off stage as an excuse for delivering an unseen diatribe of their own invention ("Come on, lads, what are we waiting for? Let's get in there and finish off Brutus and all that gang of filthy murderers..."). It is most embarrassing if the crowd noise drops and drivel like that can be heard booming across the stage.

CUEING. In Coarse theatre there is only one certain means of cueing back-stage and that is for the stage manager to walk up behind the person receiving the cue and hit them on the head when they have to begin.

How many times has one seen a cue light blinking away merrily while the lighting operator chats up a girl, or worse, empties his glass and says to the barman, "Must be getting back now, got a cue coming up." Sometimes people become mesmerised by a light and stare at it blankly; newcomers may innocently ask, "Why is that funny light going on and off?"

LIGHTING. The lighting department shares with wardrobe and sound the view that the show exists simply for their benefit. In the same way as the wardrobe mistress regards *The Miser* as an excuse for some nice frills and furbelows, so the lighting man looks at *St Joan* as merely an opportunity for some interesting flame effects.

A lighting man is not concerned with lighting either the actors or the set, but with lighting the lights, so that people will say, "What wonderful lighting."

Sometimes such praiseworthy adventure is restricted by lack of money. There are two ways of overcoming this:

1. Without any authority from the treasurer write to the lighting suppliers and hire everything under the sun from back projection equipment to pageant lamps. Then resign.

2. Keep the stage dark.

The second is the wiser course. These days, in the same way as nobody cares whether one can hear an actor, as long as you can distinguish the sound of him scratching his armpits, so nobody cares whether they *see* him or not. It is considered extremely modish if every scene takes place in utter gloom. By a strange paradox, the less light there is, the more the audience are inclined to praise the lighting staff for their cleverness.

If anyone protests, fob them off with a stream of meaningless technical drivel, such as: "Listen mate, a single modular, double thynamic board of this sort won't take any more than five hundred ohms linked in series-parallel. If I put any more on it I'll blow up the hall."

As with all backstage departments, lighting are liable to do things which are totally opposed to what is happening on stage. Askew recalls a production of *Macbeth* in which the lighting controller insisted on shining a pink spot on the ghost of Banquo. He refused all appeals from the director. "I think it looks nice," he said.

Storms and effects generally often cause trouble in the lighting department, not so much because they go wrong (which is to be expected) but because the lighting section cannot stand competition. If there is a lighting and a sound effect going on at the same time a macabre race may develop.

New companies would be well advised to use only a genuinely experienced person in charge of their lighting. Under no circumstances have anything to do with the man who says he knows a little about it, or any pamphlet entitled "How to Make your own Lighting Installations".

Watkins, who is a schoolmaster, found a do-it-yourself lighting expert from the sixth form sticking a six-inch nail in the blackened hole where the fuse had been, with the result the third act was ruined by a stench of burning rubber and clouds of evil smoke which crept from the wings. By the time the curtain call came there were only ten people left in the audience, and they were all clustered near the doors.

WARDROBE AND COSTUME. Another department whose influence is out of all proportion is the wardrobe. For practical purposes, many Coarse shows are directed by the wardrobe mistress.

For instance, it is useless for the director to say he wishes to set a play in a certain period. He may want to try a Shakespearean production in 18th-century dress and may key the whole manner of playing to that end, but if the wardrobe mistress happens to have a lot of Victorian junk lying around the production will finish up in the style of Prince Albert.

It is no use explaining the subtleties of dramatic production to a Coarse wardrobe mistress, any more than one can tell anything to the lighting man.

"Well, I think Hamlet would look very nice in that shirt John wore as Disraeli," they say when you try to explain that Hamlet is to be dressed as an army officer. And whatever arguments the director puts forward, Disraeli's shirt will make its appearance in the end. Personally, I always go to wardrobe before I even block a play, and say, "What period would you like it in?" It saves a lot of trouble.

This assumes the wardrobe department allow you to produce the play of your choice. In my experience, often they won't. If a company chooses a Molière, or anything that needs a lot of costume, they'll say it can't be done, why don't we do something simpler such as *Educating Rita*? And they always get their way. It is easier, when planning the year's programme, to go to wardrobe and ask what costumes they have got.

Law Eight of Coarse Drama is that all garments designed by a company's own staff are for being photographed in and not acting in.

I shall always remember my costume for a small part in *Othello*. It was set in a vague period which I shall call all-purpose Coarse Renaissance. My costume, however, looked like something from the Battle of Hastings. The bottom half consisted of baggy trousers such as women wear in a Turkish harem, with some tapes wound round. The upper part was simply a long cylinder.

It was all very puzzling, so I went to the wardrobe mistress and I said: "Look, this cylinder thing. Are you sure it's not part of the set?" She was very insulted, so I simply put my legs through two holes at the bottom of the cylinder, pulled it up to the chin and held it there with string.

When I walked on stage for the costume parade the designer had hysterics.

"No, no, no, Michael," she screamed. "It's upside down. You put your *arms* through the holes, not your legs. You've ruined the whole effect."

However, when I put it on the right way I found I couldn't move. So after dress rehearsal I wore the wretched thing upside down for the rest of the run and nobody complained at all.

But it is a *sine qua non* of the Coarse costume that it is impossible to move in it. Part of the reason for the poor standard of movement in amateur drama is, I am convinced, due to this. And if by some mischance the costume does allow one to move, then it will fall off at the slightest provocation.

For the great mass of Coarse actors, such as Shakespearean spear-carriers, rustics, clowns, etc., a special all-purpose Coarse garment seems to have grown up by tradition. See the photograph section.

This garment is suitable for: Old Gobbo, Young Gobbo, Pistol, Nym, Bardolph, French Prisoner, Messenger, Boatswain, Trinculo, Stephano, a Sea Captain, an Officer, Speed, Launce, Clown, Bottom, Snug, Flute, Snout, Quince, Starveling, Costard, a Forester, Adam, Dennis, Touchstone, Corin, Silvius, William, a Steward, Tranio, Biondello, Grumio, Curtis, Pedant, Autolycus, an Old Shepherd, Second Citizen of Angiers, Gaoler, Gadshill, Peto, Vintner, Drawer, First Ostler, Second Ostler, Davy, Mouldy, Shadow, Wart, Feeble, Bullcalf, Beadle, Groom, a French Sergeant, Son of the Master Gunner of Orleans, Corpse of King Henry V, Several Petitioners, a Son That Hath Killed His Father, a Father That Hath Killed His Son, First Murderer, Second Murderer, Doorkeeper to the Council Chamber, Thersites, Servant to Troilus, Servant to Paris, Servant to Diomedes,

Flaminius, Lucilius, Servilius, Caphia, Philotus, Titus, Lucius, Hortensius, Two of Timon's creditors, a Citizen of Antium, a Soothsayer, another Poet, Varro, Clotius, Claudius, Strato, Lucius, Dardanius, Pindarus, First, Second, Third, Fourth and Fifth Citizens, Pisanio, a Dutch Gentleman, Philemon, Leonine, a Pander, Boult, Fishermen, King Lear, Sampson, Gregory, Peter, Abraham, an Apothecary, Musician, Bleeding Sergeant, Drunken Porter, Ghost of Banquo, Young Siward, First Grave-digger, Second Grave-digger, Player King, Danish Captain, etc., etc., with apologies for any omissions.

The garment is a remarkable piece of costume design, since it is apparently suitable for any part over a period of 10,000 years, from the fall of Jericho to the Battle of Agincourt. It consists of a shapeless short shroud, sometimes gathered in at the waist with a bit of rope or a sword belt (N.B. Wise actors use a belt from their sister's raincoat, since most sword belts are constructed so you cannot extricate the sword). The garment is usually made of hessian, painted the appropriate colour, so the wearer comes offstage covered in dye and acquires a strange rash. For some reason, the person using it previously has always suffered from skin trouble, so it is advisable to shake it to remove any dandruff, scabs, etc. If the wearer is a soldier, he will also be given a ludicrous metal helmet, like an upturned chamber-pot.

The nether part of the all-purpose garment is tights which do not fit and which sag during performance until the crutch is around the knees. The average inside leg measurement in Coarse Acting is about six inches. If braces are worn the tights stretch until the waistband comes over your face and you have to have holes cut for the eyes.

Before being issued, the tights are specially ironed so one foot faces forward and the other backwards so there is no idea which is the front. They usually have a secret hole, which swivels round to face the audience no matter where it started.

Wearing this costume makes people give a Coarse performance. No matter what was intended, you find yourself putting on a funny walk with bent knees, twisting the face and speaking in a hoarse voice. It can't be helped – the costume takes over.

There is an equivalent all-purpose garment for women, consisting of a kind of obscene shift. This is designed so that in moments of crisis one bosom will fall out. This, too, spans 10,000 years but stretches even further than the men's and is liable to be used right up to the 19th century for peasants etc.

There is also Coarse chain mail, consisting of thick string painted silver and knitted with telegraph poles by teams of ancient women. The legs droop and become full of holes, so the audience mutter, "His armour needs darning." Be careful what is worn underneath. Sagging armour may reveal coloured boxer shorts, to the detriment of the scene.

Class distinction exists in costumes. Wardrobe will spend weeks of loving care on a few garments for the principals, and calls will be sent down during rehearsal for the leading actress to come upstairs and have her hem measured. The Coarse players, male and female, will be invited to pick their own costumes from a heap of rubbish. Hence the wardrobe mistress who inspected a Shakespeare cast looking obscene in their tights and then announced, "Jockstraps will be issued free only to those with large parts."

Finally, some warnings. First, never allow anyone to mend tights while you are wearing them, unless you are impervious to pain. In fact, never allow any garment to be mended while wearing it. Only recently, I saw a terrible accident as a result of this, when a wardrobe girl mended the dress of an actress while she was seated in a crowded dressing-room. When the actress rose to go on stage it was discovered she had been sewn to the girl next to her.

Another warning is: never lend anything to the wardrobe department. Apart from the fact the costume will come back covered in make-up and with cigarette ends in the pockets, the only thanks will be to hear people say "Where did he get that dreadful coat?"

And worse can happen. A woman was approached by a director who asked if he could borrow her velvet curtains for an 18th-century play. The good lady agreed and went to see the show. Her enjoyment was spoiled in the second act when the director himself came on wearing a velvet suit which looked

THE HUMAN CLEAT

USEFUL SOUND EFFECT
Noise of cup dropping

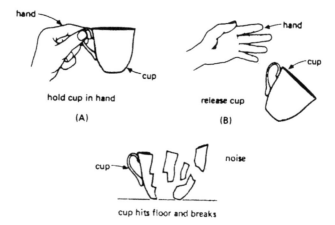

hand

cup

hold cup in hand

(A)

hand

cup

release cup

(B)

cup

noise

cup hits floor and breaks

rather familiar. After some minutes she realised it had been cut from her curtains.

Before leaving the subject of wardrobe, yet another warning must be issued: never wash your own costume.

I issue this injunction as a result of a performance of *A Midsummer Night's Dream* in which we wore extravagant costumes that had been hand-painted.

Midway through the run Titania boiled hers. It immediately turned grey and shrank to a tiny piece of material like a doll's knickers.

Since all costumes will be so constructed as to shrivel and fall apart at a touch, let wardrobe do the cleaning and take the blame. And if they do remove a costume for cleaning remember that what will return the next night will bear little relation to what you have been wearing.

PROPERTIES: Properties are never available for rehearsal of a Coarse play. It is impossible to obtain so much as a potato before the dress rehearsal.

I believe the reason is that the property department likes to spring little surprises upon the actors. They leave the unsuspecting creatures rehearsing weeks with a substitute property such as a toy pistol, and on the night produce a vast blunderbuss, which according to the script is supposed to be hidden in the waistcoat pocket.

Props are at their best over food. The cast mime a four-course meal in rehearsal, dispatching it in three minutes, of which two and a half are taken up in dialogue. At the dress rehearsal props either provide a genuine four-course meal which holds up the play for twenty minutes, or else a plastic chicken which the unhappy actor has to beat with his fork and say "Yum, yum".

On the whole, though, it is better to have a fake meal than the real thing. Apart from the fact that real fish and chips fill the theatre with a ghastly stench, the food is invariably cold. In a performance of James Saunders's one-act *Double Double*, which takes place in a bus canteen, I tried to tackle cold chips, cold fried cod in congealed fat, all covered in cold tomato sauce and washed down with cold tea. After three mouthfuls I felt so sick I nearly left the stage, but not as sick as the actor with sausages and cold custard on his plate.

Carefully test any liquid you have to drink on-stage, such as whisky, beer, tea or even lemonade. Make the first swig a cautious one. At the best, the liquid will be water, coloured with cold tea or cochineal. At the worst it may be poisonous, as when someone painted the inside of my papier-mâché mug silver and the paint came off when it was filled. It looked rather odd when I raised high my tankard in a toast and then spat all over the stage.

If cold tea is to be used, do not store it in an old whisky bottle. I say this as a result of a disastrous experience, when the props girls filled a teapot from an old whisky bottle she used to store her fake "tea". Unfortunately, it was a genuine bottle of whisky, the one the stage manager kept for a quick snort when he felt depressed. The resulting tea party on-stage was one of the most extraordinary things I've seen, with the cast taking great gulps of tea and then tottering about gasping for breath and calling for water.

SET DESIGN AND CONSTRUCTION: As stated earlier, sets are not designed to be acted upon, but are produced for the glory of the designer. As long as directors and actors know this they will save a lot of trouble and heart-burning. It is well known that sets cannot be painted until the curtain has gone up at the dress rehearsal, when a girl with a ladder will start to wander round the stage, spilling paint over everybody.

SUMMARY: I cannot conclude this chapter without the most important warning of all: never marry the ASM. This applies to both sexes.

9

Front of House and Organisation

"Sir, the gentlemen will be angry if you sit there..."
John Marston (*The Malcontent*)

**Unpleasantness in the toilets – don't shoot the reporter,
he's doing his best – regrettable outbreak of deafness
– how not to get a cup of coffee**

HOUSE MANAGER AND STEWARDS: One of the biggest joys for the connoisseur of Coarse Drama is the activities of the front-of-house staff. It is remarkable that while the actors can hardly be heard the house staff all have booming, resonant voices which they do not hesitate to use during the performance. Frequently a scene will be ruined by this sort of dialogue.

"Quiet, please, the performance has started. May I see your ticket, madam? Ah, f6 and f7? Down the left-hand aisle near the front...just a moment, sir..."

In many companies it might be a good idea to exchange the front-of-house staff with the actors, thus ensuring that at least the cast will be audible.

The duties of a Coarse house manager have little in common with those of his equivalent in the professional theatre, who appears merely to stride about in evening dress with a flower stuck in the buttonhole, making himself pleasant to Michael Billington or Peter Hall if they should happen to look in.

A Coarse house manager will find himself busy dealing with the inevitable confusion of box-office, refreshment staff and the publicity. For instance, while the posters say the curtain will rise at eight, the tickets state seven-forty-five and the stage manager says seven-thirty (the local Press have the times right but the days wrong).

In addition there is the Ninth Law of Coarse Drama to contend with. This states: "On any given night of a play there will be an overflow in the toilets."

Far from wearing the traditional evening dress and flower, a house manager would be well advised to come in overalls and rubber waders, and bring a plumber's plunger with him.

Another hazard is dealing with members of the audience who have gone to sleep. Ideally, one should have a long pole and tap them gently on the head, but if this is impossible one will just have to find an excuse for asking loudly if they are in the right seats.

Drunk members of the audience are fortunately rare, although I recall an actor who was so piqued at not being cast in a show that he got plastered on the first night and interfered with a scene by saying loudly, "Ha, ha, very funny", at all the humorous lines. Fortunately he fell asleep for the rest of the first half and did not return after the interval.

As few small venues have a stage door the house manager will find himself having to deal with would-be visitors backstage. It is best to pretend to pass on a message but in fact don't do so, as a protection to the cast. How can someone do justice to a part when she gets a message: "Your ex-husband is in the audience and asked me to tell you he will kill himself if you don't return."

The house manager, like the stage manager, will be on guard against a stream of interrupters, and will station himself at the main door to intercept them. These will range from the inevitable policeman ("Is the owner of 786 YMX here?") to drunken Irishmen trying to get in for the Shamrock Ball, and acting members of the society attempting to sneak in for nothing (actors always seem to be under the impression they do not need to buy tickets). He will also be prepared to deal with members of the cast in costume, trying to see what the production looks like from the back.

While obviously this practice must be checked – it is very disconcerting for anyone in the back row when a person leans on their seat and turning round they find themselves face to face with Sweeney Todd – stern measures are useless. The easiest way to clear a member of the cast from the auditorium is simply to say, "Aren't you due on stage in a minute?" I have seen entire armies flee for the exit at those magic words.

The last and perhaps most important duty of a Coarse house manager is to watch for the director, who will be found snooping round muttering "Oh God" occasionally. Gently lead him away and stop him from trying to climb on stage.

BOX-OFFICE: The box-office will be staffed by people incapable of counting. Either the hall will be overbooked, so twenty people are causing a din at the back trying to get in, or whole chunks of the auditorium will be deserted ("Well, I'm afraid Freda lost that part of the plan"). The only certain thing is that the number of seats in the hall will bear no relation to the squares on the plan.

The greatest menace to a box-office are the cast, who reserve whole rows for their friends and then fail to sell the tickets, so every night the box-office staff have to deal with dozens of returns. By some perversity of fate, however, if a show is a sell-out, close relations of the cast will besiege the box-office demanding admittance. It is difficult to refuse someone who shouts, "I have travelled fifty miles from Colchester to see my daughter in this play and now you won't let me in."

Sometimes a soft-hearted official gives way and by the time the relations of all the cast have arrived the hall is a mass of people fighting for seats.

REFRESHMENT STAFF: The refreshment staff, who appear to be specially trained to make a noise, are under the impression the interval is the reason for the show.

Indeed, often they are not quite certain what is going on in the hall itself. Unfortunately they are usually equally vague about their own department, with the result it can be taken as a law of Coarse Drama that refreshments are available only ten minutes after the interval.

The interval itself is marked by long queues of hungry and thirsty people waiting patiently while the refreshment staff try to coax the water to boil.

PUBLICITY MANAGER: A publicity manager's main task is to deal with the local Press. The only constant factor in this is the photographer, who will always appear punctually an hour before the dress rehearsal starts and demand that all cast immediately get into costume for the picture. As most of them haven't even arrived by then, he will seize six of the likeliest people, line them up against a half-finished piece of scenery and mow them down with his camera.

This gives small-part players a chance as the major characters are never changed in time. The photographer, who invariably has to attend another function at once, will then leave hastily without taking any details. As one who spent many years as a reporter on local newspapers, I know the routine of photographers can't be altered. If the editor can't do it, the publicity manager cannot hope to.

However, the approach of critics is less determinable. A few may have no interest in the show at all or leave at the interval. They are the best, as they will incline to praise. Encourage them by writing to say how much their report was appreciated, (although they may not thank you for this, as it means they'll have to do the ghastly job again). Have pity on the poor reporter. After all, he may have seen *Bedroom Farce* fifteen times. Refrain from telling the editor he left at the interval.

Critics who misinterpret things can be a problem, although I am grateful to the lady who described the collapse of my throne, due to defective construction, as "signalling the fall of a corrupt society." A more unfortunate gaffe was to mistake an actress of sixty-five for her thirty-year-old daughter, thinking the daughter was made up to look old. "As the grandmother," she wrote, "Sheila Middleton gave a brilliant study of old age, painfully limping about the stage with lined face, bent back and sagging breasts. She really did look hideously aged."

Some swine cut out the write-up, underlined the bit about sagging breasts, and stuck it on the mother's dressing-room mirror.*

It is a law of Coarse Theatre that at every show there will be a rumour the *Guardian* are coming (or the *Stage,* or radio or some important reviewer). Front-of-house staff go wild trying to identify the critic, only to find it was all a mistake. Don't worry. Publicity cuts both ways and critics can hurt. Indeed, some appear to enjoy doing so. The write-up which never appears may be the best write-up.

Critics could retort that if people put on untalented rubbish in public they must expect to be panned. I commend to them the tradition of Coarse Drama: "All critics are wrong, but those who praise the show have had a flash of lucidity." This equally applies to professionals.

SECRETARY: Basically there is no such thing as the secretary of an amateur theatre company because the office changes hands so frequently any occupant is always a temporary passer-by, filling in for a few weeks before the committee persuade someone else to take on the post.

The main duties of the secretary are to tone down the committee minutes (censoring such remarks as "Well, everyone knows you never could act, old boy, you're just jealous...") and to compose his letter of resignation ("Regret that after only three weeks in office must reluctantly hand over to someone with more time...").

TREASURER: People take on the treasurer's job because they wish to gain revenge on the actors and directors, whom for some reason they envy. As long as this is understood then a lot of friction will be avoided when the treasurer allows a production budget of a hundred pounds for *Bartholomew Fair* and loses a thousand on a gala dinner. However, as no one else will understand finance, there is no point in quarrelling with the treasurer. It is impossible to argue with people who use phrases like, "By writing up the fixed assets we have turned our

---

* Actually, I did it.

loss into a profit." Those of us who have simple minds in which one just adds up what was spent, adds up what was received and subtracts one from the other, are mere pawns.

PLAY SELECTION: This is best done by a small committee. As everyone will disagree with the choice of play it is better that a committee should bear the burden of criticism rather than an individual. Remember the failure of a Coarse Drama production is always blamed on the choice of play, never on the acting.

ORGANISATION OF THEATRE GROUP: Although in theory most companies are under the control of a committee, one person is often the inspiration behind a group. Coarse Actors much prefer to avoid responsibility and sit back and criticise with outbursts at the annual meeting ("Mr Chairman, when are we going to do something about the fact that all our plays are cast by a clique?").

It can be taken for granted that the annual meeting will provide the funniest performance of the year and the only time when most of the speakers will know their lines. But while a Coarse Actor should criticise freely, never make the mistake of being elected to anything.

However, a word of warning about the chairman. This post tends to go to an old acting member. At first sight one might think he accepts because of his long service to the society. But it is not so. An old actor who becomes chairman does so in the belief that it will help him get those parts he has been coveting all his life, and which up to now have eluded him. Unless watched carefully, within a few months he will have insinuated his own choice of play, insinuated his son as director of it and had himself cast in the best part, probably the juvenile lead.

SOCIAL ORGANISATION: The social side of a drama group is most important. That is all a great many of the actors and actresses come for. While formal social events tend to be the acme of dullness, the best are those unrehearsed episodes which arise spontaneously, such as we-all-hate-the-director sessions in the local pub.

After-show parties are a problem. Many shows are only remembered for the party ("Oh yes, that was the play when

John Woodward tried to strangle Fred Bloggs at the rave-up afterwards..."). Discos are only suitable if you don't want to talk or think; never believe anybody who promises to keep the music down.

There's something rather attractive about having a party on-stage and relaxing on the scene of so much tension. However, parties of this sort are inevitably ruined by a Spectre at the Feast from the stage staff, who goes about gloomily reminding people it's all right for them, but they have to clear this lot up in the morning and get all the lights down as well.

Sometimes parties are held at a private house. That's fine if everybody is invited, but I have known people who invited their cronies and left out the rest.

One problem of the private-house party is it inhibits that free, frank and usually vicious discussion of play and director which is the best part of any after-show celebration. After all, it's rather difficult to stand in someone's kitchen having another helping of their quiche and saying what a lousy director they are. However, this does not stop people doing it.

A further danger of the private house party is persons who will insist on doing their piece. Askew has actually recited "Gunga Din" fifteen times to my recollection.

It is fatal to encourage them. They will go on all night unless stopped. I remember one chap who was so persistent we seriously considered the old music-hall technique of dragging him away by means of a long stick hooked round his neck. Much better to greet the offender with a chorus of remarks like, "Don't ring us, we'll ring you" and "I wouldn't give up your day-time job yet." It sounds cruel but is kinder in the long run.

The best way to make a party go is to perform a savage skit on the play. This may be the only chance the cast have of expressing their real feelings about it.

10

Festivals and Tours

"The wind was so strong that a stage-hand had to stand behind each wing and hold it up so that it would not topple over towards the audience..." constantin Stanislavski

Alarming experience at festivals – mystery of the missing flats – appeal to Tamworth Co-operative Society – mayhem in Edinburgh – Unpleasantness in one of Her Majesty's prisons – the Unpleasantness over *Tannhäuser*

Playing away from home is a useful experience for the Coarse Actor. A strange stage, a strange audience, a strange venue all make one appreciate how good it is to come home and not have to change in a dressing-room with one mirror among 16 people.

One of the most nerve-racking types of tour is the competitive one-act festival. Troubles begin with transport. It is the Eleventh Law of Coarse Acting that properties, scenery and costumes will never arrive intact (a sub-section of the law states that the cast are quite likely not to arrive intact either). "I thought you said *you* were going to bring the pistol," is the sort of anguished howl one hears outside the hall.

I would give five pounds to know what happened to the scenery for our production of *The Dumb Waiter*. The stage manager swears that it was carefully checked and loaded on the van, yet when the vehicle arrived two flats were missing. The van doors were still locked. Who would want to steal two flats?

Even if you are lucky enough to have scenery the costumes will not all be there. Few feelings in life equal the pang of horror that goes through an actor when the skip has been emptied and his trousers still have not been found. This, of course, can make for some interesting performances. When my friend Askew's entire costume vanished he wrapped himself in two tablecloths. In view of the fact that he was supposed to be portraying the Duke of Orleans he came in for some criticism by the adjudicator, but the main thing is that the show went on.

Be careful of properties and scenery. In the confusion, as rival teams of stagehands jostle with each other, things can go astray. We once came away with a completely worthless door, labelled "Tamworth Co-operative Society Drama Group", in exchange for a marvellous flat which had been painted for us by the designer at the local rep.

As regards acting in a festival, remember the audience are not merely different from at home but actively hostile. Apart from your own tiny clique it will consist entirely of the friends and relatives of other competing societies, so don't think you're going to get away with any of those characteristic bits of business that go down so well at home. Be prepared to act in stony silence.

To this must be added a further disadvantage that the stage is strange and the festival stage manager is a saboteur in league with a rival group. I was once just about to make an entrance when one of these gentlemen seized my arm and pulled me away, saying, "You can't stand here, we've got to store a flat in this hole."

I forced my way on stage after a great struggle, protesting and shaking my fist to such an effect that the adjudicator later complimented me on my entrance. The only trouble came when I tried to go off and found the exit blocked with someone else's set.

The same law applies to the adjudication as to a Press review. If it is full of praise, take it seriously. If it is critical, ignore it.

The primary job of a director at a festival is to keep his cast off the beer. Coarse Actors go berserk away from home. As soon as they pile out of their cars, instead of examining the dressing-rooms, getting the pitch of the hall and so on, they will move into the centre of the road, sniff the air for a moment and then march into the nearest boozer.

If left there they will come back in half an hour, laughing foolishly, slurring their words, and with cans of lager sticking from their pockets. Once that happens it is as well to write off the whole production, although the cast will doubtless have a wonderful time.

TOURS: The Edinburgh Festival Fringe is one of the great experiences of touring, even though the ordeal can leave the company shattered (and broke). I shall never forget a Nottingham University student who travelled from London to see his group put on a play he'd written. He dashed straight to the hall from the train and got to his seat just after the curtain rose. Only then did he realise he was the only person in the hall. A week later he was still the only person in the audience. Nobody came to see the play. So in despair they all went home with a week to go. Every year about a dozen companies return because nobody comes to see them.

My own first venture to Edinburgh with *The Coarse Acting Show* threatened to go the same way. The caretaker, or servitor as they are quaintly called in Scotland, welcomed us by saying, "Ye'll no get any audience the first night. We had Hinge and Bracket here last year and they only got six." I didn't know at the time that Scottish servitors are a law to themselves and have been known to censor a play off their own bat. ("Ye can no have that nude scene in this hall. The lassie must clothe her wee loins.") To make matters worse, our late dress rehearsal was stopped by the police after complaints about noise, so we had to do it in mime. As the show was supposed to be funny it was rather depressing. At midnight we slunk away, defeated.

Morale was not improved next evening by having to use the gents' toilet as a dressing-room. Peering through a basement grating, one of the cast noticed a big crowd on the pavement and ran out to see what had happened. He was back immediately. "My God", he cried, "they're queuing to see us!"

We celebrated our success with a party afterwards and at 3am were demonstrating golf strokes when one of the cast got hit on the head by a backswing which knocked him out and cut him badly. For the second time in 24 hours police appeared.

The officer obviously thought it was a drunken brawl.

"Who committed the assault?" he demanded.

Our oldest actor, a respectable civil servant, stepped forward, "Well, I did actually," he stammered, "but it wasn't really an assault. He got in the way of my golf swing."

The constable looked at him cynically and then asked a question that could only have been asked in Scotland.

"Aye?" he said. "And what club did you use?"

"A five-iron actually, but does it matter?"

For one awful moment I thought the policeman was going to say, "Och, you should have used a three wood, dropping the hands down the shaft a wee," but he contented himself with saying, "It's lucky you didn't use a driver or you'd have killed him."

At 4.30 that morning I was walking up and down the casualty department of Edinburgh Royal Infirmary trying to learn the injured man's lines. The first thing he heard on recovering consciousness was me repeating them the other side of the screen and he cried out feebly, "Don't let Mike play my part... I'll do it somehow."

A good example of how the threat of losing a part will spur a Coarse Actor to any lengths. Yes, he did manage to totter on stage that evening with nine stitches in his face.

It was at Edinburgh in later years that we had an actor arrested between the dressing-room and the stage. Dressed as a terrorist, complete with machine gun, he had to run round the outside of the hall to enter through the audience, and a worthy citizen rang the police to say a man waving a gun was running around the street. On his second entrance he was intercepted and questioned, while on stage there was frantic gagging ("I think Pat should be here any minute now...").

Fortunately, the officers were sympathetic and didn't detain him. The Edinburgh Fringe owes a lot to the local police who become used to dealing with weird characters such as actors who have painted their face green and then got drunk in the Royal Mile.

Way-out shows are an essential part of the Fringe. I remember one, put on by a college group, which began with a spotlight on three heaps of fake vomit on the stage (deeply symbolic no doubt). One afternoon a drunk got in and inspired by the sight added a fourth and genuine heap. The performance was temporarily abandoned.

Avoid "missionary" tours, those where a director feels a call to take culture to the masses. Victims of this desire can include children, old age pensioners, soldiers, dementia patients and the homeless.

These directors insist on taking unsuitable plays thinking they are educational, such as a performance of *Waiting for Godot* to a group of teenage delinquents. Since the audience is unsophisticated they may not hesitate to shout out comments of which "Look behind you" is the mildest. I remember a tour of *Hamlet* where an *Ophelia/Hamlet* scene was greeted with a hoarse shout of "Shag her before she changes her mind".

I once allowed myself to be mixed up in a murder play which they took to a prison, of all places. I was playing a policeman. I have been greeted by some strange noises in my time but never has my entrance been heralded by anything like the sound that came as I walked on stage in the recreation room. I very nearly walked straight off again. Every time I opened my mouth to speak there was a near riot.

The back-stage staff, who were mostly prisoners, explained that the men were a little upset because a mass-break-out had been foiled the day before and the ringleaders were languishing in solitary. I told the governor the prisoner working the lights seemed an awfully pleasant chap, and the governor said he recently stabbed someone with a dinner knife, being given to uncontrollable fits of violence.

"You were lucky he didn't have a go at you when he saw your copper's uniform," he added jovially.

Despite all this, I would prefer to act in a prison than in a school. Give me the honest criminal any day in preference to children.

An audience of children is simply a collection of malevolent minds waiting for an excuse to make a noise. Unfortunately Coarse Acting offers them plenty of opportunity for this. Where an adult audience will merely stir uncomfortably at a prompt, an audience of children will say loudly, "He's forgotten his lines, he can't remember what he's got to say next, he'll have to ask that lady peering round the edge of the curtain..." It's almost impossible to stand up to that sort of thing.

It is dangerous to act to children in the round, or without the protection of a solid proscenium arch. Even in normal conditions things are bad enough, what with senior boys smoking in the back row and making amorous experiments with senior girls, and youngsters talking and chewing sweets in front, but without a proscenium the wretches have an opportunity to get at the actor physically.

During *St Joan* I watched with horror as a little infant got up and caught hold of the butt end of somebody's spear. There was a tug-of-war which only ended when the distraught actor jabbed the spear violently backwards into the child's ribs.

Afterwards the child's mother wrote to the director and complained her son had a great weal on his ribs, but the director had had enough by then and replied his only regret was that it wasn't the child's head.

Sometimes children will even talk to the actors. It is a little disconcerting when a tiny hand tugs at one's cloak and a voice pipes up, "Mister, do you know there's a hole in your sock?"

It is fatal to ignore the voice, because the questioner becomes even more persistent until he is answered. And it is equally fatal to engage the child in conversation, because the conversation never finishes.

Another difficulty of touring is that the stage is often improvised in a place not normally used for dramatic performances, such as a hospital ward or a school gymnasium.

It was this that led to the Unpleasantness at Perivale, where playing in a school I swept superbly off with the intention of returning from the other side two minutes later. I walked out of the tiny wings and through a door, turned right, and went through another door which should have led to a passage at right angles to the stage.

I was rather surprised to find myself in a classroom where evening students were studying life drawing. After a moment's embarrassment I retired and took the next door on the right, which turned out to be the boiler house. The man stoking the furnace summed up the situation neatly when he said: "Ah mate, you're in the wrong room. You want the next door but two down the corridor."

By this time I was becoming rather worried. I ran to the door he indicated. It was a Scottish dancing class. I honestly think I would still be floating round that wretched school if I hadn't heard laughter in the distance. I knew that sound. It was the noise made by a group of children when an actor fails to appear. Guided by the noise, which was increasing in intensity, I ran through a door into the playground and saw the lights of the hall. It was no time for niceties. I pulled open an emergency exit at the back and dashed in, spattered with rain.

Occasionally the unexpected happens on tour and one is embarrassed by the lavishness of the stage. Some years ago Askew and I played in a production of *Twelfth Night* which toured Germany and Austria. We took with us a ludicrous assembly of cheap wood and nuts and bolts, which was our all-purpose "set". When erected it formed a square bower, rather like a small public convenience, and when dismantled it fell apart into a collection of pieces which would never fit the bag in which they were carried.

We duly arrived at the Opera House in Klagenfurt, Austria. The stage of this is rather formidable, about the size of Wembley Stadium. We had a matinée for local schools, sandwiched between a performance by a professional German company of *Die Walküre* the previous night and *Tannhäuser* the same evening.

The stage manager and the director arrived with our bag of little sticks and dumped it on the stage. It looked rather lonely. A troop of twenty stage-hands appeared, headed by Herr Stage Direktor.

"Please," he enquired, "you wish us to erect your set immediately?"

"Good heavens, no," said our director, who was a rather fussy man. "We couldn't trust you with a set like this. I'm the only person who knows how to put it together, old boy. Unless you do it in a certain order you get a bit left over at the end."

Herr Direktor looked put out.

"It is good," he said, with an expression which indicated that it wasn't, and he marched away his stage staff.

The performance went on and ended. Immediately the ninety-foot curtain had fallen Herr Direktor marched on stage.

"Please", he said, "will you have the goodness to remove your scenery as we wish immediately to set *Tannhäuser* for the performance in an hour's time."

Our director became flustered. "I'm doing it as fast as I can," he said stiffly. "You must remember that unless it's done in a certain way we can't pack it."

Herr Direktor made a strange sign. Twenty men emerged from the shadows.

Next moment our little pavilion was whirling round on the revolve while the director, who was off the revolving section, chased after it. As he did so, *Tannhäuser* descended from the flies, nearly braining him. He finally caught up with our set after it had travelled about a hundred yards, but before he could start work they began to set scenery all round it.

It was two hours before the director crept out into the street, dragging his little canvas bag of bits. Next day, when we arrived in Vienna, we found a piece of wood was missing. We wrote to Herr Direktor, but he never returned it.

Some companies take shows on tour to hospitals. This does guarantee a passive audience, most of them too numbed by weeks in bed to make any reaction at all, although domestic disturbances, such as faint cries for a bedpan, can be disturbing during a performance.

Not that I see why sick or elderly people should have Coarse Acting inflicted upon them without any choice in the matter. One of the great Drama fallacies is that people who are old or ill have lost their critical faculties and are grateful to have any sort of tripe served up.

I shall not forget chairing an Old Time Music Hall at a club for the disabled, at which the audience showed their opinion by starting to wheel invalid chairs all over the hall to talk to their friends. Some of them were kind enough to wave a stick at me and shout "Don't mind us – just carry on" as they whizzed past. Another offered me a cup of tea just before the punch-line of my only joke. I don't blame them a bit. No one has a right to impose a bad show on the helpless.

11

'Tis Pity She's the Merry Wife of Henry VI
(Part One)

Being a risible Elizabethan tragi-comedy-history, dedicated to whomever happens to be in power at present, and specially written with the intention of affording opportunities for a Coarse Actor to play seven different parts, all of increasing moronity.

N.B. Application to perform this piece should be made to Samuel French in the usual way. However, it's not really written to be staged. For a fuller acting version see *Henry the Tenth* (**Part Seven**) in *Coarse Acting Two*, **one of the four volumes of Coarse plays published by Samuel French, details of which are given at the end of this book.**

ACT ONE

Scene One

A room in the castle of St Albans. Flourish. Enter hautboys.

Enter **KING** *with* **DARLINGTON, DONCASTER, RETFORD, GRANTHAM, NEWARK, PETERBOROUGH, WELWYN, HITCHIN** *and their trains. Enter* **COARSE ACTOR** *carrying flagon of wine. While they are all dressed in the usual Shakespearean odds-and-ends the* **COARSE ACTOR** *stands out by reason of his stock small part costume, the crowning glory of which is an obscene pair of old tights whose crutch is somewhere around his knees. The procession goes round and round meaninglessly. Exeunt.*

Scene Two

Another part of St Albans. Flourish. Enter **KING** *with* **LORDS** *and* **ATTENDANTS** *as before, minus cupbearer.*

KING My Lord of Darlington, what news from Scotland?

DARLINGTON My liege, there is even at this moment an emissary arrived from Ross.

There is a long pause.

(savagely) My liege, there is *even at this moment* an emissary arrived from Ross.

The **COARSE ACTOR** *arrives with a kilt tied hastily over his tights.*

KING Thy panting breath betrays thy haste. I like it not. Say, tell me what thy tidings are.

CA My liege—

KING Know thou, thou scurvy messenger, that we

Have fifteen nights now watched Orion turn

His vasty arc in yon benighted sky

And fifteen times have heard bad news from Ross.

What can'st thou bring to ease our royal burden?

CA *(in atrocious Scottish accent)* My liege, I bring thee nothing but defiance, The rebel host, consuming all before it, doth already—

The **KING** *gives a growl of fury and rises and picks up the messenger by the equivalent of his lapels. He shakes him savagely and then flings him to the ground in an immense cloud of dust which has arisen from his costume. He lies grovelling.*

KING Thou naughty messenger!

These tidings that thou bringst mislike us well

And for the evil news that thou hast brought

I'll have thee flogged throughout the town tonight.

Thus shalt thou know defiance is not made

So easily against our royal person.

Go drag him hence and beat him mightily.

CA My liege, I – whurp...

He is dragged out with unnecessary force.

KING Go, Darlington, and cousin Grantham too.

Get thee ten thousand men and meet me here

Tomorrow. Let all bend unto his task

Until the rebels do for mercy ask.

His voice rises to an Olivier-type shriek.

His crown falls off.

Exeunt.

Scene Three

Another room in the castle at St Albans. Enter the QUEEN, *with fifteen attendants, one of whom is the* COARSE ACTOR *who has got rid of his kilt but probably retains vestiges of his Scottish costume elsewhere. He is carrying a property lute with slack strings made of string. He plays this furiously. Suddenly, the noise of a lute bursts forth at deafening amplification just as he stops playing. He starts again hurriedly. The lute sound stops suddenly. The* COARSE ACTOR *carries on vigorously.*

QUEEN Oh woe! Alack the day!

ALL Oh woe! Alack the day! Rhubarb! Woe the day! Alack the woe! Rhubarb! etc.

Exeunt for no reason at all, QUEEN *weeping. Last out is the* COARSE ACTOR *who has now got his hand firmly trapped in the hole of the lute.*

ACT TWO

Scene One

A street in St Albans. Enter **FIRST CLOWN** *and* **COARSE ACTOR** *as* **ASSISTANT CLOWN** *or all-purpose Shakespearean stooge. He is walking with a strange gait that suggests an internal injury, because he thinks this is how clowns should walk.*

FIRST CLOWN By the Mass thou look'st as sad as a quondam neat's tongue dried at Blackfriars, the one the French tailor could not stomach.

CA Aye, marry and amen.

They pause, because the director has told them this is funny. It is, however, received in silence, except for the rustle of programmes as the audience look to see if this pair are supposed to be comics.

FIRST CLOWN I will cheer thee with some merry jests. Tell me, good neighbour Clodpony, why is a codpiece like a candlemaker?

CA Nay, I know not.

FIRST CLOWN Thou makest light of the jest; and doth not a candlemaker make light also? Therefore thou art a very candlemaker indeed. Ergo, thou art a codpiece.

The **CA** *bursts into unconvincing and exaggerated laughter.*

CA And were I a codpiece I should know where to hide my light.

He clutches his loins. They fall about with simulated mirth.

FIRST CLOWN Prithee, dost think the King will defeat the rebels?

CA Aye, he were no King otherwise.

FIRST CLOWN That were a royal remark. And were the King no King he would be a rebel indeed. *(He pauses for a laugh which never comes).* But come old Clodpony, answer me this. What is it that hath a horn and hath not a horn?

He places his fingers on his forehead in the traditional horn sign.

CA God's sonties, but I know not.

FIRST CLOWN Stir thy wits.

CA Alas, I have none.

FIRST CLOWN Why, the answer is: a cuckold when Michaelmas falls on a Thursday.

CA But why on Thursday?

FIRST CLOWN Mass, I know not.

CA No more I prithee, lest I injure myself with laughing at the subtlety of thy jests.

He rocks with immoderate laughter which is interrupted by the **FIRST CLOWN** *savagely beating him with his bladder.*

FIRST CLOWN But let's away. We must to St. Albans to see the King.

Both exit, gibbering and mowing.

There is the sound of people leaving the audience.

Scene Two

The rebel camp near St Albans. Enter **WOLVERTON, BLETCHLEY, MILTON KEYNES, RUGBY, NUNEATON, STAFFORD** *and* **CREWE,** *muttering.*

BLETCHLEY Therefore, brothers, unto our several tasks. And ere yon Phoebus thrice five times has passed over this wrinkled orb we call the earth.

The King shall know the mettle of our minds.

MILTON KEYNES Aye, and perchance the metal of our swords.

Everyone falls about with mirth except the audience.

BLETCHLEY Why, that's my brother Milton Keynes. I do know the sharpness of thy wit and relish thee the more withal.

NUNEATON The King will not relish us, my lord.

STAFFORD He will find us too hot for his relish.

RUGBY Too hot? Nay then we shall pepper him.

There is a positive explosion of mirth at this hilarious exchange. The mirth, however, is confined to the stage. The numbed audience sit in silence.

BLETCHLEY Where's Wolverton?

RUGBY Somewhere in Buckinghamshire.

BLETCHLEY Enough, coz. Be not a spendthrift with thy jests lest haply some may return to thee. Is Wolverton here?

There is a heaving at the back of the throng and the **COARSE ACTOR** *bursts into view, having made several unavailing efforts to burst through previously. He has now put on a lord's surcoat but cannot hide the obscene tights which are his trademark. He still wears the lute.*

CA Here, my lord.

BLETCHLEY Then hie thee to St Albans. Carry our defiance
to the King.

CA I will with upmost speed, my lord. *(Exeunt)*

ACT THREE

Scene One

The KING's camp. A tucket sounds.

KING Who is this man with looks so wild who gurdily approaches us?

Enter CA.

CA My liege I bring letters from Bletchley.

KING The very name is hideous in mine ears! Vile Bletchley! O, perfidious, evil man! I'll none of them. And thou return to him and tell him so, thou wart.

During the last two lines he delivers the now-familiar assault upon the COARSE ACTOR, *hurling him savagely to the ground. The* COARSE ACTOR *limps off.*

A LORD What now, my liege?

KING To arms, that's all a man can do.

ALL Aye, to arms, it's all a man can do.

KING If fate should choose we are to die today...

ALL Aye, today, fate, choose etc.

KING Let's die at least with armour on our backs.

ALL Aye, with armour, on our backs, at least...

KING Let not the sun shine more
If St Albans in rebel hands is sure.

ALL St Albans, in rebel hands, sure...

The KING *charges off followed by the army, some of whom trip over their spears.*

Scene Two

Part of the battle. The main battle is going on in the dressing-room where the **COARSE ACTOR** *has wiped off his earlier make-up and exchanged it for a scrofulous beard, as he is now on the* **KING**'s *side (temporarily). Over his tights he has pulled knitted chainmail trousers of thick string, which have split up the back in a rather obscene fashion. He reaches the wings with some difficulty, as an army is trying to rush off stage, and finds he has forgotten his sword. He hopefully seizes a passing weapon and runs on stage with it.*

BLETCHLEY Our cause doth prosper well. I'll make up to my brother Wolverton.

CA Hold, rebel.

BLETCHLEY Who art thou?

He looks at his wrist.

CA I am Sir John Thomas Erpingham-Blunt. No, I am Lord Wellingborough. I think.

BLETCHLEY Then defend thyself.

They fight. This consists of continually crossing swords and grunting. Occasionally they lock hilts and in one daring move **BLETCHLEY** *beats at the* **CA**'s *shield. Suddenly the* **CA** *holds out his left arm,* **BLETCHLEY** *passes his sword under the armpit and the* **CA** *drops, gurgling horribly.*

CA Oh, I die.

He remembers to expire behind a piece of scenery, crawls off, changes shields and returns at once.

BLETCHLEY Then farewell, good Wellingborough. I'll to my brother Stafford.

Enter **DARLINGTON**.

DARLINGTON The King doth labour mightily. I'll rest me here
and see what I can see.

Enter **COARSE ACTOR** *after changing his shield.*

CA Stand!

DARLINGTON Thou rebel dog, I'll teach thee tell me stand.
Sayst stand dost thou? Then stand upon thy stand or I'll
unstand thee.

He waves his sword vaguely in the air.

CA Oh, I am dust.

He dies (again).

*Nevertheless he manages to crawl off stage, where,
flinging a cloak over his armour, he ties himself up
with rope and waits to be dragged on stage as a rebel
prisoner. Unfortunately no one appears to do this, so
when the cue comes he slinks on by himself, holding
the rope out horizontally in front of him to indicate
he is being led.*

KING *(recovering from his surprise)* What surly men are these?

NEWARK The rebel prisoners, my liege.

KING Their very sight offends me. I will none
Of them. Go hang them all with utmost speed
About St Albans market square. Cut off
Their rebellious noses on the way
And beat their naughty persons mightily.

Exit **COARSE ACTOR** *being beaten.*

KING News have we that the weasel French,
consumed with envy at our royal success is e'en

against us now in arms. Thus meet it is

that we with speediness do take our leave.

The dead in pious clay we'll cover

And then immediately proceed to Dover.

ALL On toward Dover ho!

Exeunt in procession. Just as they are leaving, the CA, *who has changed again, enters at the tail of the queue.*

CA On toward Dover, ho!

He passes into the wings where he immediately starts to collect the tea money.

The End

Epilogue

Spoken by the Author

The Critic sitting in his slippered ease
Says we who please to write must write to please.
Though now it's easier to fill the belly
By being rude to people on the Telly.

I'll none of this; and should my book offend
(Especially in reference to my friends)
I penitent will always be: I swear it,
But if the cap fits, chum, then you must wear it.

PLAYS FOR COARSE ACTORS

There are four volumes of one-act plays for Coarse Actors and they are all available from Samuel French Ltd.

FOUR PLAYS FOR COARSE ACTORS
Containing:

Streuth is a crime story which even Agatha Christie would never have dared to write.

II Fornicazione is a grim tale of operatic adultery, poison and mayhem.

A Collier's Tuesday Tea combines the kitchen sink with the coal-mine, and with an irreverent glance at D.H. Lawrence.

All's Well That Ends As You Like It ("from an idea by William Shakespeare" and set in "the Forest of Solihull") pushes the genius of the Bard to its utmost limits, while managing to filch lines from most of his own plays.
ISBN 978-0-573-00008-9

THE COARSE ACTING SHOW 2
(Further Plays for Coarse Actors)
Containing:

Moby Dick is a rather over-ambitious attempt to reduce the epic novel (685 pages long) into a series of quick-fire scenes.

The Cherry Sisters, a hitherto undiscovered fragment of Chekhov, is a desperately sincere piece, with a real tear-jerker of an ending, spoiled only by the fact that someone has to die standing up in order to cope with a faulty prop.

Last Call for Breakfast is full of symbolism, a short avant-garde piece made shorter by the simple mischance of one of the actors getting himself in the wrong position during a blackout.

Henry the Tenth (Part Seven) is a rarely-performed masterpiece (from a suggestion by William Shakespeare) with battle scenes of which the Bard would have been proud.
ISBN 978-0-573-10005-5

THE THIRD GREAT COARSE ACTING SHOW
Containing:
A Fish in Her Kettle. It is the simple lack of a door handle which causes the disaster, as most of the cast find themselves trapped on stage when the door jams.
Present Slaughter collapses because of one unlucky slip by the leading man, who cuts his wrist when he collides with a tableful of glasses.
The Vagabond Prince is an all-purpose Coarse Musical, with a roistering chorus of gypsies and earthy tavern men and women.
Stalag 69 is, according to the director, "a seminal investigation into the relationship between man and war", a noble concept somewhat marred by the fact that the set is upside down for the first run-through, and collapses completely during the second, revealing the stage staff enthusiastically producing a startling range of live sound effects.
Julius and Cleopatra, a Roman spectacular, illustrates two of the Laws of Coarse Acting: one, that every person in a Coarse crowd is hideously deformed or crippled for some reason, and two, that when stabbed, all pain is always felt in the bowels, no matter where the wound is!
ISBN 978-0-573-00030-0

COARSE ACTING STRIKES BACK
Containing:
Trapped! In a send-up of a traditional English thriller, the cast find themselves not trapped when the over-energetic lead actor knocks down doors that were meant to be locked.
Oedocles, King of Thebes. The spoof Greek tragedy presents a fine example of a Coarse Acting script, enhanced by Coarse management and direction.
Pride at Southanger Park. Written by Rupert Bean and edited by Michael Green, this is supposedly an adaptation of a long-lost Jane Austen novel, presenting a naturally developing and utterly hilarious set of acting disasters.

Cinderella. The Prince is a stout older woman, the cat anything but catlike, and the slipper fits the Ugly Sisters. Not to mention a transformation scene which doesn't work and a disastrous attempt to fly the Good Fairy.
ISBN 978-0-573-10009-3

UMLAUT, PRINCE OF DÜSSELDORF
Imagines a hapless and incompetent theatre company attempting a condensed version of Hamlet. The ghost is determined to ruin all of Umlaut's best speeches while Hildegard (Coarse Ophelia) keeps forgetting that she's supposed to be dead.
ISBN 978-0-573-12291-0

HAGGARD – AN ENTERTAINMENT
by Eric Chappell based on characters created by Michael Green.
ISBN 978-0-573-11165-5